Linux Command Line

First Edition
Sarful Hassan

Preface

This book provides a comprehensive guide to mastering the Linux command line, tailored for beginners as well as more experienced users who wish to deepen their knowledge of Linux. By exploring the fundamental concepts and command-line tools in Linux, readers will gain hands-on skills for navigating, managing files, handling system information, and much more. This book is designed to be a practical reference that equips readers with the knowledge necessary to utilize the Linux command line efficiently.

Who This Book Is For

This book is intended for anyone interested in understanding and using the Linux command line effectively. Whether you're a student, a developer, a system administrator, or a hobbyist, this book will provide valuable insights into Linux. No prior knowledge of Linux is assumed, making this book ideal for beginners. Experienced users will also find it beneficial for mastering advanced topics.

How This Book Is Organized

The book is organized into several chapters, each focusing on a specific area of the Linux command line:

- Introduction and basics of Linux navigation and file manipulation.
- Advanced topics such as text processing, system monitoring, networking, and disk management.
- In-depth sections on permissions, software management, automation, development tools, debugging, and system analysis.
- Chapters on shell scripting, system performance, network management, and storage utilities.

Each chapter builds on previous knowledge, helping you progressively develop skills in Linux.

What Was Left Out

While this book covers a broad range of Linux topics, some highly specialized commands and topics have been omitted to keep the focus on essential command-line skills. However, additional resources and links are provided for further exploration of advanced topics.

Release Notes

This edition includes updated chapters on system monitoring, network management, and virtualization, reflecting the latest advancements in Linux command-line tools. Additional examples and updated exercises enhance the learning experience.

Notes on the First Edition

The first edition of this book introduced foundational Linux concepts, which are now expanded upon in this edition. Feedback from the first edition readers has been invaluable in refining and expanding the content to make it even more user-friendly.

MechatronicsLAB Online Learning

MechatronicsLAB is dedicated to providing high-quality resources for learners at all levels. Visit mechatronicslab.net for more online resources and updates.

How to Contact Us

For feedback, questions, or further information, feel free to reach out:

- Email: mechatronicslab@gmail.com
- Website: mechatronicslab.net

Acknowledgments for the First Edition

We extend our gratitude to all contributors, reviewers, and users of the first edition. Your feedback has been invaluable in shaping this edition. Special thanks to the MechatronicsLAB community for their ongoing support.

Copyright

This book is copyrighted by MechatronicsLAB. All rights reserved. No part of this book may be reproduced, stored, or transmitted without prior written permission.

Disclaimer

The information provided in this book is for educational purposes only. While every effort has been made to ensure accuracy, MechatronicsLAB assumes no responsibility for any errors or omissions. Readers are advised to consult additional sources when applying the information in professional environments.

Table of Contents

Chapter – 1 Introduction to Linux and the Command Line

Chapter Overview

Linux is a powerful and flexible operating system that powers everything from servers to smartphones. A key feature of Linux is its command line interface (CLI), which allows users to interact with the system by typing commands. This chapter introduces Linux, explains the different distributions, compares the graphical user interface (GUI) and command line interface (CLI), and covers essential topics like navigating the terminal, using shortcuts, and the different types of shells available.

Chapter Goal

- Learn the basics of Linux, including its history and distributions.
- Understand the difference between GUI and CLI and why the command line is useful.
- Learn how to open and navigate the terminal, essential rules for using the command line, and shortcuts.
- Get familiar with common command line shells, such as Bash and Zsh.

1.1 Brief History of Linux

Linux began in 1991 as a personal project by Linus Torvalds, a Finnish student who wanted to create a free and open-source operating system. Inspired by UNIX, a powerful operating system used in large institutions, Linus Torvalds aimed to develop an OS that could run on personal computers. Since then, Linux has grown through contributions from developers worldwide and is now a stable and versatile OS used in everything from smartphones (like Android) to web servers.

Key Points in Linux History

- **1991**: Linus Torvalds releases the first version of the Linux kernel.
- **1992**: Linux is released under the GNU General Public License (GPL), making it free and open-source.

- **2000s**: Linux gains popularity in server environments due to its stability, security, and flexibility.
- **Today**: Linux is widely used across different industries, from cloud computing to mobile devices.

1.2 Understanding Linux Distributions

A **Linux distribution** (or "distro") is a version of Linux that includes the Linux kernel, system tools, and additional software, all packaged together to create an operating system. Different distributions are designed for different purposes, and each has its unique features and community support.

Popular Linux Distributions

1. **Ubuntu**: Known for its user-friendliness and extensive software repository, Ubuntu is a great choice for beginners.
2. **Debian**: Known for stability and reliability, Debian is often used on servers.
3. **Fedora**: Sponsored by Red Hat, Fedora is popular among developers and provides cutting-edge software.
4. **Arch Linux**: A lightweight, flexible distribution for advanced users who want to customize their environment.
5. **CentOS**: A stable, enterprise-focused distribution often used in server environments.

Choosing a Linux distribution depends on your needs, preferences, and experience level. Most distributions come with either a graphical desktop environment or the option to use the command line exclusively.

1.3 GUI vs. CLI: Why Use the Command Line?

Linux provides both a graphical user interface (GUI) and a command line interface (CLI). The GUI allows users to interact with the system through windows, icons, and menus, while the CLI allows direct interaction through typed commands.

GUI (Graphical User Interface)

- Easy to use, especially for beginners.
- Ideal for tasks like web browsing, document editing, and basic file management.
- Relies on visual interaction, such as clicking and dragging.

CLI (Command Line Interface)

- More powerful and flexible for certain tasks.
- Allows advanced users to automate tasks through scripts.
- Uses fewer resources, making it ideal for older or lower-spec hardware.

Why Use the Command Line?

The CLI can be faster and more efficient for certain tasks, such as file management, installing software, or troubleshooting.
Additionally, the CLI allows for scripting and automation, making it ideal for repetitive tasks. Many Linux power users prefer the command line because it gives them more control over the system.

1.4 Opening and Navigating the Terminal

The **terminal** is the program that lets you access the command line on Linux. When you open a terminal, you're interacting with a shell (like Bash) that reads and executes commands.

Opening the Terminal

- **Ubuntu and Debian**: Press Ctrl + Alt + T or find "Terminal" in the Applications menu.
- **Fedora**: Press Ctrl + Alt + T or find "Terminal" in the Activities overview.
- **Arch Linux**: Look for "Terminal" in the Applications menu or install a terminal emulator if needed.

1.5 Basic Rules for Using the Command Line

Here are some key rules to keep in mind when using the command line:

1.5.1 Think Before You Execute

Commands run instantly, so double-check before pressing Enter. Some commands can change or delete files, so it's important to understand what each command does.

1.5.2 Use Sudo with Caution

sudo (superuser do) gives you administrative privileges, allowing you to make system-wide changes. Always use it carefully, as incorrect commands with sudo can cause serious issues.

1.5.3 Be Careful with File Deletion

Deleting files with `rm` or directories with `rm -r` is permanent and cannot be undone. Always verify the file name and location before deleting.

1.5.4 Use Help and Man Pages

If you're unsure about a command, use `man` to read its manual:

```
man command_name
```

Alternatively, you can use `command --help` for quick information.

1.5.5 Stay Organized in Your Directories

Keep your files organized and try not to make changes outside your **home directory** (usually `/home/username`) until you are familiar with the system.

1.5.6 Keep Commands Simple at First

Stick to basic commands as you're learning, such as `ls`, `cd`, and `pwd`. This helps you build confidence before moving on to more complex commands.

1.6 Using Shortcuts in the Command Line

Shortcuts make using the command line faster and easier. Here are a few essential shortcuts:

1.6.1 Tab Completion

- **Tab**: Use the Tab key to complete file or folder names automatically. Start typing a name, press Tab, and the terminal will try to complete it for you.

1.6.2 Navigating Command History

- **Up Arrow**: Scroll through previous commands.
- **Down Arrow**: Move forward through the command history.

1.6.3 Clearing the Screen

- **Ctrl + L**: Clear the screen without deleting any previous output. This is helpful to keep the screen organized.

1.6.4 Canceling Commands

- **Ctrl + C**: Cancel a running command. Useful if a command is taking too long or you typed it by mistake.

1.6.5 Moving the Cursor
- **Ctrl + A**: Jump to the start of the line.
- **Ctrl + E**: Jump to the end of the line.

1.6.6 Deleting Text
- **Ctrl + U**: Delete everything from the cursor's position to the start of the line.
- **Ctrl + K**: Delete from the cursor to the end of the line.

These shortcuts help make the command line experience more efficient and manageable.

1.7 Common Shells: Bash, Zsh, and Others

The **shell** is the program that processes commands typed into the terminal. Different shells have slightly different features and syntax. Here are a few of the most popular shells in Linux:

1.7.1 Bash (Bourne Again Shell)
- **Most Common**: Bash is the default shell on many Linux distributions, including Ubuntu and Fedora.
- **Scripting Support**: Bash is popular for scripting because of its robust support for automation and custom scripts.
- **Easy to Use**: Most Linux tutorials and resources use Bash, so it's easy to find help and examples.

1.7.2 Zsh (Z Shell)
- **Enhanced Features**: Zsh includes additional features like better auto-completion, spell-checking, and customization options.
- **Highly Customizable**: Many users prefer Zsh for its customization and themes, especially with the **Oh My Zsh** framework, which makes setup easy.
- **Popular in MacOS**: Zsh is the default shell on recent versions of macOS, making it common across Linux and macOS users.

1.7.3 Fish (Friendly Interactive Shell)
- **User-Friendly**: Fish is designed to be user-friendly with intuitive syntax and strong auto-suggestions.

Chapter – 2 Basic Navigation & Structure

Chapter Overview

This chapter covers essential Linux commands for navigating and managing the filesystem. These commands allow you to move between directories, view directory contents, create and delete directories, and visualize directory structures in tree format. Understanding these commands is fundamental for anyone working with a Linux or Unix-based system, as it enables efficient file and directory management.

Chapter Goal

- Learn to navigate the filesystem and understand the current directory.
- Understand how to view, create, and remove directories.
- Visualize directory structures to gain a better understanding of file organization.

Syntax Table

Serial No	Command	Syntax	Simple Example
1	List Contents	`ls [options] [directory]`	`ls -l /home`
2	Change Directory	`cd [directory]`	`cd Documents`
3	Print Working Directory	`pwd`	`pwd`
4	Make Directory	`mkdir [directory_name]`	`mkdir new_folder`
5	Remove Directory	`rmdir [directory_name]`	`rmdir old_folder`
6	Display Directory Tree	`tree [directory]`	`tree /home/user`

Topic Explanations

1. ls - List Directory Contents

What is ls

The ls command lists the contents of a directory, displaying files and subdirectories. It's one of the most commonly used commands for checking the contents of a directory.

Use Purpose

- **View Files and Folders**: Lists all files and folders in the current or specified directory.
- **View Additional Details**: With options, displays permissions, file sizes, modification dates, and ownership information.

Syntax

```
ls [options] [directory]
```

Syntax Explanation

- **ls**: The basic command to list directory contents.
  - **[options]**: Optional parameters to modify the output. Common options include:
    - **-l**: Displays details in long format, showing permissions, owner, size, and date modified.
    - **-a**: Includes hidden files (files starting with .).
    - **-h**: Makes file sizes human-readable (e.g., 10K instead of 10240 bytes).
  - **[directory]**: Specifies the directory to list. If omitted, ls defaults to the current directory.

Simple Code Example

```
ls -lh /home/user
```

Code Example Explanation

1. **Lists contents** of the /home/user directory.
2. **Uses -l** to show additional details (long format) and -h for human-readable file sizes.
3. Displays permissions, ownership, size, and date modified for each item.

Common Errors and Solutions
- **Error**: `ls: cannot access 'non_existent_dir': No such file or directory`
  - **Solution**: Double-check the directory name or path to ensure it exists before using `ls`.

Notes
- The `ls -l` command displays file permissions in the first column. For example, `drwxr-xr-x` indicates a directory (d) with permissions `rwx` for the owner, `r-x` for the group, and `r-x` for others.
- Combining `ls` with other commands, like `ls | grep 'pattern'`, allows for filtering of output to find specific files.

Warnings
- Attempting to list a directory that doesn't exist will result in an error message.

---

2. cd - Change Directory

What is cd
The `cd` (change directory) command moves you from one directory to another within the filesystem.

Use Purpose
- **Navigate Between Directories**: Moves to a specified directory to access files or subdirectories.
- **Quick Directory Access**: Allows easy and efficient movement across the directory structure.

Syntax
```
cd [directory]
```

Syntax Explanation
- **cd**: Command to change the current directory.
  - **[directory]**: Specifies the path to the directory you want to move into. Common options include:
    - `..`: Moves up one level to the parent directory.
    - `~`: Moves to the user's home directory.
    - `-`: Switches to the previous directory.

Simple Code Example

```
cd Documents
```

Code Example Explanation

1. **Navigates** to the Documents directory from the current location, allowing access to files or further subdirectories within it.

Common Errors and Solutions

- **Error**: bash: cd: non_existent_dir: No such file or directory
  - **Solution**: Use ls to list available directories and ensure the specified directory exists.

Notes

- Using cd .. moves up one directory level, while cd - returns you to the last accessed directory.
- cd alone, without arguments, brings you back to your home directory.

Warnings

- Specifying a directory that doesn't exist will produce an error.

---

3. pwd - Print Working Directory

What is pwd

The pwd (print working directory) command displays the current directory's full path.

Use Purpose

- **Verify Current Location**: Helps confirm your exact location within the filesystem.
- **Avoid Navigation Errors**: Ensures you're in the correct directory before running other commands.

Syntax

```
pwd
```

Syntax Explanation

- **pwd**: Outputs the absolute path of the current directory, providing context for subsequent commands.

Simple Code Example

```
pwd
```

Code Example Explanation
1. **Displays** the current directory's full path, confirming your location in the filesystem.

Common Errors and Solutions
- **Error**: None typically occurs, as pwd doesn't require arguments or additional options.

Notes
- Useful in scripts and for tracking locations within deeply nested directories.
- Especially helpful when moving through multiple directories to avoid confusion.

Warnings
- Use pwd to confirm your location before running commands that depend on a specific directory.

---

4. `mkdir` - Make Directories

What is `mkdir`

The `mkdir` (make directory) command creates new directories, allowing you to organize files by grouping them into folders.

Use Purpose
- **Organize Files**: Allows you to create folders for grouping related files together.
- **Set Up Directory Structure**: Useful for creating project directories with multiple folders.

Syntax

```
mkdir [directory_name]
```

Syntax Explanation
- **mkdir**: Command to create a new directory.
  - **[directory_name]**: Specifies the name of the new directory. This can be a relative or absolute path. If it includes multiple levels, the parent directories must already exist unless the -p option is used.

Additional option:
- **-p**: Creates parent directories if they do not already exist, useful for creating nested folders.

Simple Code Example

```
mkdir new_folder
```

Code Example Explanation

1. **Creates** a directory named `new_folder` in the current directory, allowing for organized file storage.

Common Errors and Solutions

- **Error**: `mkdir: cannot create directory 'existing_folder': File exists`
  - ○ **Solution**: Use a unique directory name or delete the existing folder if it's no longer needed.

Notes

- `mkdir -p /path/to/dir` allows creating nested directories without causing an error if a parent folder is missing.
- Use `mkdir` to structure projects by creating folders for documents, code files, and resources.

Warnings

- Avoid using a name that conflicts with existing files to prevent errors.

---

5. rmdir - Remove Empty Directories

What is rmdir

The `rmdir` (remove directory) command deletes empty directories from the filesystem.

Use Purpose

- **Remove Unused Folders**: Helps keep the filesystem clean by deleting unused directories.
- **File Management**: Useful for cleaning up empty folders in a project.

Syntax

```
rmdir [directory_name]
```

Syntax Explanation

- **rmdir**: Command to remove an empty directory.
  - ○ **[directory_name]**: Specifies the name or path of the empty directory to remove.

Simple Code Example

```
rmdir old_folder
```

Code Example Explanation

1. **Deletes** the `old_folder` directory if it is empty, helping reduce clutter in the filesystem.

Common Errors and Solutions

- **Error**: `rmdir: failed to remove 'dir': Directory not empty`
  - ○ **Solution**: Use `rm -r dir` to delete non-empty directories with caution.

Notes

- Use `rmdir` only on empty directories; otherwise, it will return an error.
- For deleting non-empty directories, consider using `rm -r`, but be cautious as it removes all files and subdirectories within.

Warnings

- Attempting to remove a non-empty directory with `rmdir` will cause an error.

---

6. `tree` - Display Directory Structure in Tree Format

What is `tree`

The `tree` command displays the contents of a directory in a tree-like format, showing files and subdirectories in a hierarchical structure.

Use Purpose

- **Visualize Directory Structure**: Provides an organized view of files and folders.
- **Assess Directory Contents**: Helpful for understanding the layout of large or complex directories.

Syntax

```
tree [directory]
```

Syntax Explanation

- **tree**: Command to display the directory structure in tree format.

o **[directory]**: Specifies the directory to visualize. Defaults to the current directory if omitted.

Additional options:

- **-L n**: Limits the depth of the displayed tree structure to n levels, making large directories easier to view.
- **-d**: Displays directories only, omitting files for a cleaner view.

Simple Code Example

```
tree -L 2 /home/user
```

Code Example Explanation

1. **Displays** a tree structure for /home/user, showing only the top two levels, making it easier to view the directory organization.

Common Errors and Solutions

- **Error**: tree: command not found
    - **Solution**: Install tree using sudo apt install tree on Linux.

Notes

- tree is a helpful command for quickly assessing the structure of a directory, especially in large projects with multiple nested folders.

Warnings

- Displaying an entire directory tree for a deep structure can result in a large output. Use -L to limit the depth if necessary.

Chapter – 3 File Manipulation

Chapter Overview

This chapter covers essential Linux commands for creating, removing, copying, moving, and linking files and directories. Mastery of these commands is crucial for managing files effectively in a Linux environment, allowing you to organize, backup, and manage file structures with ease.

Chapter Goal

- Understand the fundamental commands for creating, removing, copying, and moving files and directories.
- Learn how to create symbolic links to files, enabling easier access and management.
- Gain proficiency in handling files and directories using the command line.

Syntax Table

Serial No	Command	Syntax	Simple Example
1	Create an Empty File	`touch [filename]`	`touch file.txt`
2	Remove Files/Directories	`rm [options] [filename]`	`rm file.txt`
3	Copy Files/Directories	`cp [options] [source] [destination]`	`cp file.txt backup/`
4	Move/Rename Files	`mv [source] [destination]`	`mv file.txt documents/`
5	Create Symbolic Links	`ln -s [target] [link_name]`	`ln -s /path/to/file link_name`

Topic Explanations

1. touch - Create an Empty File

What is touch

The touch command is primarily used to create empty files or update the timestamp of an existing file without modifying its content.

Use Purpose

- **Create Empty Files**: Allows quick creation of new files for use in scripts or as placeholders.
- **Update File Timestamps**: Modifies the last accessed or modified time of an existing file.

Syntax

```
touch [filename]
```

Syntax Explanation

- **touch**: Command to create a new file or update an existing file's timestamp.
  - **[filename]**: Specifies the name of the file to create or modify. Can include a relative or absolute path.

Simple Code Example

```
touch notes.txt
```

Code Example Explanation

1. **Creates** an empty file named notes.txt in the current directory if it doesn't already exist.
2. If notes.txt exists, updates the file's modification timestamp without altering its content.

Common Errors and Solutions

- **Error**: touch: cannot touch 'filename': Permission denied
  - **Solution**: Ensure you have write permissions in the directory or use sudo for administrative access.

Notes

- The touch command can be used to create multiple files at once, e.g., touch file1.txt file2.txt.
- Updating timestamps is helpful when managing automated backups or testing file synchronization.

2. rm - Remove Files or Directories

What is `rm`

The `rm` (remove) command deletes files and directories permanently. It's essential for managing and cleaning up files but should be used cautiously to avoid accidental data loss.

Use Purpose

- **Delete Files**: Removes unwanted files from the filesystem.
- **Remove Directories**: Deletes entire directories and their contents if specified.

Syntax

```
rm [options] [filename]
```

Syntax Explanation

- **rm**: Command to remove files or directories.
  - ○ **[options]**: Modifies the command's behavior. Common options include:
    - ■ **-r**: Recursively deletes a directory and all its contents.
    - ■ **-f**: Forces deletion without prompting for confirmation.
    - ■ **-i**: Prompts for confirmation before each deletion.
  - ○ **[filename]**: Specifies the file or directory to delete.

Simple Code Example

```
rm -i file.txt
```

Code Example Explanation

1. **Deletes** the `file.txt` file.
2. Uses `-i` to prompt for confirmation, preventing accidental deletion.

Common Errors and Solutions

- **Error**: `rm: cannot remove 'file': No such file or directory`
  - ○ **Solution**: Verify the file's existence and correct path before running rm.

Notes

- Use rm -r with caution, especially in directories containing many files or critical data.
- The -f (force) option overrides prompts but should be used carefully to avoid unintentional deletions.

Warnings

- Files removed with rm cannot be recovered. Double-check the filename and path before executing.

---

3. cp - Copy Files and Directories

What is cp

The cp (copy) command duplicates files or directories, creating identical copies in a specified location.

Use Purpose

- **Create File Backups**: Makes a copy of files or directories to ensure data safety.
- **Duplicate Files**: Allows for file distribution or organizational purposes.

Syntax

```
cp [options] [source] [destination]
```

Syntax Explanation

- **cp**: Command to copy files or directories.
  - **[options]**: Modifies the command's behavior. Common options include:
    - **-r**: Copies directories recursively, including all files and subdirectories.
    - **-i**: Prompts before overwriting an existing file at the destination.
    - **-u**: Copies only when the source file is newer than the destination file or when the destination file is missing.
  - **[source]**: Specifies the file or directory to copy.
  - **[destination]**: Specifies the target location where the copy will be saved.

Simple Code Example

```
cp -r /project/documents /backup
```

Code Example Explanation
1. **Copies** the entire `documents` directory and its contents from `/project` to `/backup`.
2. Uses `-r` to ensure all subdirectories and files within `documents` are copied.

Common Errors and Solutions
- **Error**: `cp: cannot stat 'file': No such file or directory`
  - **Solution**: Verify the source file's existence and correct path.

Notes
- cp allows multiple files to be copied at once by specifying multiple source files followed by the target directory.
- Overwriting files without `-i` will proceed without warning; consider using `-i` in important cases.

Warnings
- Use the `-r` option only when necessary, as it can lead to copying large amounts of data unintentionally.

---

4. mv - Move or Rename Files and Directories

What is mv
The mv (move) command relocates files or directories to a different location or renames them without duplicating.

Use Purpose
- **Move Files**: Transfers files or directories to a new location.
- **Rename Files**: Changes the name of a file or directory without altering its contents.

Syntax
```
mv [source] [destination]
```

Syntax Explanation
- **mv**: Command to move or rename files and directories.
  - **[source]**: Specifies the file or directory to move or rename.
  - **[destination]**: Specifies the target location or the new name for the file or directory.

Simple Code Example

```
mv report.txt archived_report.txt
```

Code Example Explanation

1. **Renames** the report.txt file to archived_report.txt in the current directory, allowing for more descriptive naming.

Common Errors and Solutions

- **Error**: mv: cannot move 'file': No such file or directory
    - **Solution**: Ensure the source file exists and that the path is correct.

Notes

- Using mv with an existing file in the destination will overwrite it without warning; consider using -i for confirmation.
- If the source and destination are in the same directory, mv acts as a renaming tool.

Warnings

- Double-check file paths to avoid accidental data overwrites when moving files to a destination with existing files.

---

5. ln - Create Symbolic Links Between Files

What is ln

The ln (link) command creates hard or symbolic (soft) links between files. Symbolic links, similar to shortcuts, point to another file or directory.

Use Purpose

- **Create Shortcuts**: Enables easier access to files located in other directories.
- **Maintain Consistency**: Links allow multiple references to a file without duplicating it.

Syntax

```
ln -s [target] [link_name]
```

Syntax Explanation

- **ln**: Command to create links between files.
    - **-s**: Specifies a symbolic link. Without -s, a hard link is created instead.

- [target]: The file or directory that the link points to.
- [link_name]: The name of the link being created.

Simple Code Example

```
ln -s /var/www/html/project project_link
```

Code Example Explanation

1. **Creates** a symbolic link named `project_link` that points to `/var/www/html/project`, allowing easier access to the `project` directory.

Common Errors and Solutions

- **Error**: `ln: failed to create symbolic link 'link_name': File exists`
  - **Solution**: Specify a unique link name or delete the existing link if it's no longer needed.

Notes

- Symbolic links can point to files across filesystems, while hard links must reside within the same filesystem.
- Removing a symbolic link does not affect the target file.

Warnings

- Deleting the target file breaks the link; be cautious when managing linked files.

Chapter – 4 File Viewing & Content Display

Chapter Overview

This chapter covers essential Linux commands for viewing file contents and searching within files or across the filesystem. Mastering these commands enables efficient content viewing, pattern searching, and file location, making it easier to manage and analyze text files, logs, and large data files.

Chapter Goal

- Learn to display and navigate file contents using different commands.
- Understand how to search within files for specific patterns.
- Gain proficiency in locating files by name or attribute.

Syntax Table

Serial No	Command	Syntax	Simple Example
1	Display File Contents	`cat [filename]`	`cat file.txt`
2	View File Interactively	`less [filename]`	`less file.txt`
3	View File Page by Page	`more [filename]`	`more file.txt`
4	Display First Part of File	`head [options] [filename]`	`head file.txt`
5	Display Last Part of File	`tail [options] [filename]`	`tail file.txt`
6	Search for Patterns	`grep [options] "pattern" [filename]`	`grep "error" logfile.txt`

| 7 | Search for Files by Attribute | `find [path] [options] [expression]` | `find / -name "file.txt"` |
| 8 | Quickly Find Files by Name | `locate [options] [pattern]` | `locate file.txt` |

Topic Explanations

1. cat - Display File Contents

What is cat

The `cat` (concatenate) command displays the contents of a file or concatenates multiple files to output their combined content.

Use Purpose

- **View File Contents**: Quickly displays the entire contents of a file.
- **Combine Multiple Files**: Concatenates files for output in sequence.

Syntax

```
cat [filename]
```

Syntax Explanation

- **cat**: Command to display or concatenate file contents.
  - **[filename]**: Specifies the file(s) to display. Multiple filenames can be provided to concatenate.

Simple Code Example

```
cat file.txt
```

Code Example Explanation

1. **Displays** the content of `file.txt`, outputting it in full on the terminal.

Common Errors and Solutions

- **Error**: `cat: file.txt: No such file or directory`
  - **Solution**: Verify the filename and path to ensure the file exists.

Notes

- cat is useful for quickly viewing small files. For large files, consider using less or more for better navigation.

Warnings

- Be cautious when using cat with large files as it will display the entire content, potentially causing scrolling or performance issues.

2. less - View File Contents Interactively

What is less

The less command allows you to view file contents interactively, making it ideal for large files. It doesn't load the entire file into memory, making it faster and more efficient.

Use Purpose

- **View Large Files**: Efficiently displays large files without loading the entire content.
- **Interactive Navigation**: Supports scrolling, searching, and jumping within the file.

Syntax

```
less [filename]
```

Syntax Explanation

- **less**: Command to interactively view file contents.
  - **[filename]**: Specifies the file to display.

Simple Code Example

```
less file.txt
```

Code Example Explanation

1. **Opens** file.txt in interactive mode.
2. Allows **scrolling** with arrow keys or **searching** using / for text within the file.

Common Errors and Solutions

- **Error**: less: No such file or directory
  - **Solution**: Check the file's path or name before executing less.

Notes

- Press q to quit `less` and return to the terminal.
- For searching within `less`, press / followed by the search term.

Warnings

- Unlike `cat`, `less` opens files in read-only mode, so changes are not saved.

---

3. `more` - View File Contents Page by Page

What is `more`

The `more` command displays file content page by page, making it suitable for viewing large files without scrolling through the entire output.

Use Purpose

- **Page-by-Page Viewing**: Breaks large files into pages for easier reading.
- **Basic Navigation**: Provides limited navigation compared to `less`.

Syntax

```
more [filename]
```

Syntax Explanation

- **more**: Command to display file contents page by page.
  - **[filename]**: Specifies the file to view.

Simple Code Example

```
more file.txt
```

Code Example Explanation

1. **Displays** the content of `file.txt` page by page.
2. Press the **spacebar** to advance to the next page.

Common Errors and Solutions

- **Error**: `more: file.txt: No such file or directory`
  - **Solution**: Verify the file's name and path.

Notes

- For files that fit within a single page, `more` shows the entire content without pagination.

4. head - Display the First Part of a File

What is head

The head command displays the first part of a file, with the default showing the first 10 lines.

Use Purpose

- **Preview File Content**: View the beginning of a file to assess its contents.
- **Limit Output**: Show only a specified number of lines.

Syntax

```
head [options] [filename]
```

Syntax Explanation

- **head**: Command to display the start of a file.
  - **[options]**: Commonly used options include:
    - **-n**: Specifies the number of lines to display (e.g., head -n 5).
  - **[filename]**: Specifies the file to display.

Simple Code Example

```
head -n 5 file.txt
```

Code Example Explanation

1. **Displays** the first 5 lines of file.txt, providing a quick preview of the file's start.

Common Errors and Solutions

- **Error**: head: cannot open 'file.txt': No such file or directory
  - **Solution**: Ensure the filename and path are correct.

Notes

- The -n option allows you to customize the number of lines shown.

Warnings

- head is limited to the start of the file; use tail to see the end.

5. `tail` - Display the Last Part of a File

What is `tail`

The `tail` command displays the last part of a file, with the default showing the last 10 lines.

Use Purpose

- **View Recent Data**: Useful for viewing recent logs or the end of large files.
- **Monitor Real-Time Logs**: Can continuously display new lines appended to a file.

Syntax

```
tail [options] [filename]
```

Syntax Explanation

- **tail**: Command to display the end of a file.
  - ○ **[options]**: Commonly used options include:
    - ■ **-n**: Specifies the number of lines to display (e.g., `tail -n 5`).
    - ■ **-f**: Follows the file in real-time, displaying new lines as they're added.
  - ○ **[filename]**: Specifies the file to display.

Simple Code Example

```
tail -n 5 file.txt
```

Code Example Explanation

1. **Displays** the last 5 lines of `file.txt`, often used to see the most recent entries.

Common Errors and Solutions

- **Error**: `tail: cannot open 'file.txt': No such file or directory`
  - ○ **Solution**: Verify that the file exists and that the path is correct.

Notes

- `tail -f` is commonly used to monitor log files in real-time.

Warnings

- Using `tail -f` on a large, active file can consume significant resources.

6. grep - Search for Patterns in Files

What is grep

The grep command searches files for lines containing a specific pattern, making it a powerful tool for finding data in text files.

Use Purpose

- **Search Within Files**: Finds lines matching a specific pattern.
- **Filter Data**: Useful for extracting specific information from large files.

Syntax

```
grep [options] "pattern" [filename]
```

Syntax Explanation

- **grep**: Command to search for patterns within files.
  - o **[options]**: Modifies the search behavior. Common options include:
    - ■ **-i**: Ignores case in search.
    - ■ **-r**: Searches recursively in directories.
    - ■ **-n**: Displays line numbers with matched lines.
  - o **"pattern"**: The string or regular expression to search for.
  - o **[filename]**: Specifies the file(s) to search.

Simple Code Example

```
grep -i "error" logfile.txt
```

Code Example Explanation

1. **Searches** for the word "error" in logfile.txt, ignoring case differences.

Common Errors and Solutions

- **Error**: grep: file.txt: No such file or directory
  - o **Solution**: Check the file path or ensure the file exists before searching.

Notes

- Regular expressions enhance grep's power, enabling complex pattern matching.

Warnings

- Using grep with -r in large directories can result in high resource consumption.

7. find - Search for Files by Name or Attribute

What is find

The find command searches for files and directories based on attributes like name, type, size, or modification date.

Use Purpose

- **Locate Files by Attribute**: Finds files based on attributes such as name or date modified.
- **Flexible Searches**: Allows complex searches with multiple criteria.

Syntax

```
find [path] [options] [expression]
```

Syntax Explanation

- **find**: Command to search for files based on specified criteria.
  - ○ **[path]**: Specifies the directory to search in (e.g., /home/user).
  - ○ **[options]**: Modifies the search. Common options include:
    - ■ **-name**: Searches by filename.
    - ■ **-type**: Specifies file type (f for file, d for directory).
    - ■ **-size**: Searches by file size.
  - ○ **[expression]**: Defines the search criteria (e.g., -name "*.txt").

Simple Code Example

```
find / -name "file.txt"
```

Code Example Explanation

1. **Searches** the entire filesystem for a file named file.txt.

Common Errors and Solutions

- **Error**: find: '/path': Permission denied
  - ○ **Solution**: Use sudo find for administrative privileges, if needed.

Notes

- `find` is powerful but can be resource-intensive; specify narrower paths to optimize performance.

Warnings

- Searching from the root directory (`/`) can take time; use specific paths where possible.

8. `locate` - Quickly Find Files by Name

What is `locate`

The `locate` command quickly finds files by name using a prebuilt database, making it faster than `find` for name-based searches.

Use Purpose

- **Quick File Search**: Efficiently searches files by name.
- **Frequent Searches**: Ideal for routine searches with an updated database.

Syntax

```
locate [options] [pattern]
```

Syntax Explanation

- **locate**: Command to search for files using the system's database.
    - ○ **[options]**: Common options include `-i` to ignore case.
    - ○ **[pattern]**: Specifies the filename or part of the name to search for.

Simple Code Example

```
locate file.txt
```

Code Example Explanation

1. **Searches** the database for `file.txt`, outputting all matching file paths.

Chapter – 5 Text Processing

Chapter Overview

This chapter covers essential Linux commands for processing and manipulating text files. These commands allow users to output, count, sort, filter, extract, and transform text in various ways. Basic text processing commands are useful for organizing and analyzing text, while advanced commands like sed and awk allow for complex text manipulations and data extraction.

Chapter Goal

- Understand basic text processing commands to output and manipulate text.
- Learn advanced commands for transforming text, performing search and replace, and data extraction.
- Gain skills to process and analyze structured data, extract specific text, and work with large files.

Syntax Table

Seria l No	Command	Syntax	Simple Example
1	Output Text	echo [text]	echo "Hello World"
2	Count Lines, Words, Characters	wc [options] [filename]	wc -l file.txt
3	Sort Text	sort [options] [filename]	sort file.txt
4	Filter Repeated Lines	uniq [options] [filename]	uniq file.txt
5	Extract Columns	cut [options] [filename]	cut -d ',' -f 1 file.csv

6	Find and Replace Text	`sed [options] 's/old/new/' [filename]`	`sed 's/error/fix /' file.txt`
7	Extract and Report Data	`awk [options] 'pattern {action}' [filename]`	`awk '{print $1}' file.txt`
8	Translate Characters	`tr [options] set1 set2`	`tr 'a-z' 'A-Z' < file.txt`
9	Number Lines	`nl [options] [filename]`	`nl file.txt`

Topic Explanations

1. echo - Output Text to Terminal

What is echo

The echo command outputs text to the terminal. It is commonly used in shell scripts for displaying messages or values of variables.

Use Purpose

- **Display Text**: Outputs simple text to the terminal.
- **Print Variable Values**: Useful in scripts for printing variable content.

Syntax

```
echo [text]
```

Syntax Explanation

- **echo**: Command to output text.
  - **[text]**: The text to display. Can be enclosed in quotes for strings or include variables.

Simple Code Example

```
echo "Hello World"
```

Code Example Explanation

1. **Displays** the text "Hello World" in the terminal as output.

Common Errors and Solutions
- **Error**: If special characters are interpreted unexpectedly, use escape sequences (e.g., echo `"Hello \$USER"`).

Notes
- **Environment Variables**: Use $VARIABLE_NAME to display environment variables.

Warnings
- Avoid using special characters without escaping, as they may behave unexpectedly.

---

2. wc - Count Lines, Words, and Characters
What is wc
The wc (word count) command provides counts for lines, words, and characters in a file.

Use Purpose
- **Analyze File Content**: Quickly see the number of lines, words, or characters in a file.
- **Data Validation**: Useful for checking file lengths in scripts.

Syntax
```
wc [options] [filename]
```
Syntax Explanation
- **wc**: Command to count lines, words, or characters.
  - **[options]**: Specifies the count type:
    - **-l**: Counts lines.
    - **-w**: Counts words.
    - **-c**: Counts characters.
  - **[filename]**: The file to analyze.

Simple Code Example
```
wc -l file.txt
```
Code Example Explanation
1. **Counts** the lines in `file.txt`, outputting the line count in the terminal.

Common Errors and Solutions
- **Error**: wc: file.txt: No such file or directory
  - **Solution**: Check the filename and path to ensure the file exists.

Notes

- Combine multiple options, e.g., `wc -lw file.txt` to see line and word counts.

Warnings

- Be aware of file sizes; counting large files may take time.

---

3. `sort` - Sort Text Alphabetically or Numerically

What is `sort`

The `sort` command sorts lines in a file alphabetically or numerically.

Use Purpose

- **Alphabetical or Numerical Sorting**: Sorts text for easy viewing or analysis.
- **Data Organization**: Organizes lines in ascending or descending order.

Syntax

```
sort [options] [filename]
```

Syntax Explanation

- **sort**: Command to sort lines.
  - ○ **[options]**: Customizes sorting behavior:
    - ■ **-n**: Sorts numerically.
    - ■ **-r**: Reverses the order.
    - ■ **-u**: Removes duplicate lines.
  - ○ **[filename]**: The file to sort.

Simple Code Example

```
sort -n file.txt
```

Code Example Explanation

1. **Sorts** `file.txt` numerically by each line's content.

Common Errors and Solutions

- **Error**: Sorting large files can use considerable memory.
  - ○ **Solution**: For large files, consider using `sort -S [size]`.

Notes

- Sort by columns with -k option, e.g., `sort -k 2 file.txt`.

Warnings

- Sorting with insufficient memory may slow down your system.

---

4. uniq - Filter Out or Show Repeated Lines

What is uniq

The uniq command filters out duplicate lines in a sorted file or highlights repeated lines.

Use Purpose

- **Remove Duplicates**: Shows unique lines by default.
- **Highlight Repeats**: Identifies repeated lines for analysis.

Syntax

```
uniq [options] [filename]
```

Syntax Explanation

- **uniq**: Command to filter duplicates.
  - ○ **[options]**: Configures the output:
    - ■ **-c**: Counts duplicates.
    - ■ **-d**: Displays only repeated lines.
  - ○ **[filename]**: The sorted file to process.

Simple Code Example

```
uniq -c file.txt
```

Code Example Explanation

1. **Counts** duplicate lines in file.txt, showing occurrences for each line.

Common Errors and Solutions

- **Error**: uniq works only on sorted data.
  - ○ **Solution**: Use sort before uniq.

Notes

- **Common Pair**: Combine sort | uniq to sort and filter in one step.

Warnings

- Unsorted files may yield inaccurate results with uniq.

---

5. cut - Extract Specific Columns or Fields

What is cut

The cut command extracts specified fields or columns from a file, useful for CSV and tabular data.

Use Purpose

- **Field Extraction**: Retrieves specific columns from structured text.
- **Data Parsing**: Ideal for processing delimited files.

Syntax

```
cut [options] [filename]
```

Syntax Explanation

- **cut**: Command to extract fields or columns.
  - **[options]**: Customizes the extraction:
    - **-d**: Specifies the delimiter (e.g., -d ',' for CSV).
    - **-f**: Indicates the field(s) to extract (e.g., -f 1).
  - **[filename]**: The file to process.

Simple Code Example

```
cut -d ',' -f 1 file.csv
```

Code Example Explanation

1. **Extracts** the first column from file.csv, using a comma as the delimiter.

Common Errors and Solutions

- **Error**: Incorrect delimiter specification.
  - **Solution**: Confirm the delimiter type used in the file.

Notes

- Use -f 1,2 to select multiple fields (e.g., columns 1 and 2).

Warnings

- Specifying an incorrect delimiter may lead to unexpected results.

6. sed - Stream Editor for Finding and Replacing Text

What is sed

The sed (stream editor) command is used to find and replace text in files, making it ideal for batch text processing.

Use Purpose

- **Find and Replace**: Replaces specific text patterns in a file.
- **Stream Processing**: Processes text without modifying the original file unless specified.

Syntax

```
sed [options] 's/old/new/' [filename]
```

Syntax Explanation

- **sed**: Command to edit text in a stream.
    - **[options]**: Common options include:
        - **-i**: Modifies the file in place.
    - **s/old/new/**: Replaces "old" with "new".
    - **[filename]**: The file to process.

Simple Code Example

```
sed 's/error/fix/' file.txt
```

Code Example Explanation

1. **Replaces** the first occurrence of "error" with "fix" in each line of file.txt.

Common Errors and Solutions

- **Error**: Syntax errors in the pattern.
    - **Solution**: Double-check the syntax of the replacement command.

Notes

- Use -i for in-place editing to save changes directly to the file.

Warnings

- Be cautious with -i as it modifies files permanently.

---

7. awk - Data Extraction and Reporting Tool

What is awk

The awk command is a powerful text processing tool used for data extraction, pattern scanning, and reporting.

Use Purpose

- **Pattern Matching**: Filters data based on patterns.
- **Data Reporting**: Outputs selected fields, ideal for tabular data.

Syntax

```
awk [options] 'pattern {action}' [filename]
```

Syntax Explanation

- **awk**: Command to process text by matching patterns and executing actions.
    - **[options]**: Common options include -F for field separators.
    - **pattern**: Defines the data to match.
    - **{action}**: Specifies the action to take (e.g., {print $1}).
    - **[filename]**: The file to process.

Simple Code Example

```
awk '{print $1}' file.txt
```

Code Example Explanation

1. **Prints** the first column of file.txt, often used for structured text.

Common Errors and Solutions

- **Error**: Incorrect field specification.
    - **Solution**: Confirm the data structure and use correct field numbers.

Notes

- awk can handle complex expressions and is useful for structured data analysis.

Warnings

- Incorrect syntax may produce unexpected outputs; verify patterns and actions.

---

8. tr - Translate or Delete Characters

What is tr

The tr (translate) command translates or deletes specified characters, commonly used for character-based text processing.

Use Purpose

- **Character Replacement**: Replaces one set of characters with another.

- **Delete Characters**: Removes specific characters from text.

Syntax

```
tr [options] set1 set2
```

Syntax Explanation

- **tr**: Command to translate or delete characters.
  - ○ **set1**: Characters to translate or delete.
  - ○ **set2**: Replacement characters.

Simple Code Example

```
tr 'a-z' 'A-Z' < file.txt
```

Code Example Explanation

1. **Converts** lowercase to uppercase in `file.txt` by translating character sets.

Common Errors and Solutions

- **Error**: Input redirection errors.
  - ○ **Solution**: Ensure `tr` is used with proper redirection (< or |).

Notes

- `tr` works on standard input/output, often paired with < for file input.

Warnings

- Translation set lengths must match for accurate replacement.

---

9. nl - Number Lines of Files

What is nl

The `nl` command adds line numbers to the lines in a file.

Use Purpose

- **Number Lines**: Adds line numbers to text output.
- **Formatting**: Useful for organizing code or structured files.

Syntax

```
nl [options] [filename]
```

Syntax Explanation

- **nl**: Command to number lines.
  - ○ **[options]**: Configures line numbering (e.g., -ba to number all lines).
  - ○ **[filename]**: The file to process.

Simple Code Example

```
nl file.txt
```

Code Example Explanation

1. **Adds line numbers** to each line in `file.txt`, displaying them alongside text.

Common Errors and Solutions

- **Error**: File not found.
  - o **Solution**: Check that the file exists and path is correct.

Notes

- `nl` is helpful for scripts where line referencing is necessary.

Warnings

- Avoid using with binary files; `nl` is for text files only.

Chapter – 6 System Monitoring & Information

Chapter Overview

This chapter covers essential commands for monitoring system information and managing processes on a Linux system. These commands allow you to view system information, monitor resource usage, and manage running processes effectively. Understanding these commands is crucial for system administrators and users managing server resources or troubleshooting system performance issues.

Chapter Goal

- Learn commands to retrieve system information such as uptime, disk usage, and memory usage.
- Understand how to monitor active processes and system resource consumption.
- Gain skills to manage and terminate processes effectively.

Syntax Table

Serial No	Command	Syntax	Simple Example
1	Print System Information	uname [options]	uname -a
2	Show System Uptime	uptime	uptime
3	Show Disk Space Usage	df [options]	df -h
4	Display Memory Usage	free [options]	free -h
5	Display Active Processes	top	top
6	Enhanced Process Viewer	htop	htop

7	Display Current Processes	`ps [options]`	`ps aux`
8	Terminate a Process	`kill [PID]`	`kill 1234`
9	Terminate Processes by Name	`pkill [process_name]`	`pkill firefox`

Topic Explanations

1. uname - Print System Information

What is uname

The uname command displays basic information about the system, such as the operating system, kernel version, and machine architecture.

Use Purpose

- **System Identification**: Helps identify the OS, kernel, and system architecture.
- **Troubleshooting**: Useful for determining system compatibility and kernel-related issues.

Syntax

```
uname [options]
```

Syntax Explanation

- **uname**: Command to display system information.
  - ○ **[options]**: Modifies the output:
    - ■ **-a**: Displays all available information.
    - ■ **-r**: Shows the kernel release version.
    - ■ **-m**: Displays the machine hardware name.

Simple Code Example

```
uname -a
```

Code Example Explanation

1. **Displays** detailed information about the system, including the OS name, kernel version, and architecture.

Common Errors and Solutions
- **Error**: None typically occurs with `uname`.

Notes
- This command provides an overview of system properties but does not show specific resource usage.

Warnings
- Use `uname -r` to specifically check kernel version if troubleshooting compatibility issues.

---

2. `uptime` - Show How Long the System Has Been Running

What is `uptime`

The `uptime` command shows how long the system has been running, the number of active users, and the load average.

Use Purpose
- **Monitor System Uptime**: Useful for tracking system stability.
- **Analyze Load Average**: Provides a quick snapshot of system load over different intervals.

Syntax
```
uptime
```

Syntax Explanation
- **uptime**: Command to display system uptime, user count, and load averages.

Simple Code Example
```
uptime
```

Code Example Explanation
1. **Outputs** the system uptime, number of active users, and the 1, 5, and 15-minute load averages.

Common Errors and Solutions
- **Error**: None typically occurs with `uptime`.

Notes
- **Load Average**: Values greater than the number of CPU cores indicate high load.

Warnings
- Uptime alone does not provide a breakdown of resource usage.

3. df - Show Disk Space Usage

What is df

The df (disk free) command displays the amount of disk space available on the filesystem, showing usage and free space for each mounted partition.

Use Purpose

- **Monitor Disk Usage**: Check available and used disk space across mounted filesystems.
- **System Health Check**: Identify storage bottlenecks or partitions close to capacity.

Syntax

```
df [options]
```

Syntax Explanation

- **df**: Command to show disk space usage.
  - ○ **[options]**: Configures the output:
    - ■ **-h**: Displays sizes in human-readable format (e.g., MB, GB).
    - ■ **-T**: Shows filesystem type.

Simple Code Example

```
df -h
```

Code Example Explanation

1. **Displays** disk usage in a human-readable format, showing each partition's usage and available space.

Common Errors and Solutions

- **Error**: None typically occurs with df.

Notes

- Use df -h frequently to monitor disk space, especially on servers and production environments.

Warnings

- Running low on disk space can impact system performance and functionality.

4. free - Display Memory Usage

What is free

The free command shows the system's memory usage, including RAM and swap memory.

Use Purpose

- **Monitor Memory Usage**: Quickly check the total, used, and free memory.
- **System Health Check**: Helps assess if the system has sufficient memory resources.

Syntax

```
free [options]
```

Syntax Explanation

- **free**: Command to display memory usage.
  - **[options]**: Configures the output:
    - **-h**: Displays memory sizes in human-readable format.
    - **-m**: Shows memory in MB.

Simple Code Example

```
free -h
```

Code Example Explanation

1. **Displays** total, used, and available memory in a human-readable format.

Common Errors and Solutions

- **Error**: None typically occurs with free.

Notes

- Regularly check memory usage to avoid high swap utilization and potential performance degradation.

Warnings

- Low free memory may cause applications to slow down or crash.

5. top - Display Active Processes and Resource Usage

What is top

The top command provides a dynamic view of active processes, displaying real-time CPU, memory usage, and process details.

Use Purpose

- **Monitor Processes**: View resource usage by active processes.
- **Analyze System Load**: Identify processes consuming high CPU or memory.

Syntax

```
top
```

Syntax Explanation

- **top**: Command to display real-time process and system resource information.

Simple Code Example

```
top
```

Code Example Explanation

1. **Displays** a live view of processes, including CPU and memory usage, sorted by CPU usage by default.

Common Errors and Solutions

- **Error**: None typically occurs with top.

Notes

- Press q to exit top.
- Press k within top to kill a process by entering its PID.

Warnings

- Running top for extended periods can increase system load slightly.

---

6. htop - Enhanced Interactive Process Viewer

What is htop

The htop command is an enhanced version of top, providing a more user-friendly, interactive view of active processes with color-coded resource usage.

Use Purpose

- **Enhanced Process Monitoring**: View processes with better organization and navigation.
- **Resource Management**: Easily sort and filter processes by usage type.

Syntax

```
htop
```

Syntax Explanation

- **htop**: Command to launch an enhanced interactive process viewer.

Simple Code Example

```
htop
```

Code Example Explanation

1. **Launches** htop with a colorful, user-friendly view of processes and resource usage.

Common Errors and Solutions

- **Error**: htop: command not found
  - **Solution**: Install htop using your package manager (e.g., sudo apt install htop).

Notes

- Use F3 to search and F9 to kill processes within htop.

Warnings

- As an advanced viewer, htop may not be pre-installed on all systems.

---

7. ps - Display Current Processes

What is ps

The ps command shows a snapshot of active processes, providing static process information.

Use Purpose

- **List Running Processes**: Provides detailed information on active processes.
- **Process Management**: Identifies processes by user or ID.

Syntax

```
ps [options]
```

Syntax Explanation

- **ps**: Command to display process information.
    - ○ **[options]**: Modifies output, with common options including:
        - ■ **aux**: Lists all processes in a detailed view.
        - ■ **-e**: Shows all processes.

Simple Code Example

```
ps aux
```

Code Example Explanation

1. **Lists** all active processes with detailed information, including process ID (PID), user, CPU, and memory usage.

Common Errors and Solutions

- **Error**: None typically occurs with ps.

Notes

- ps aux | grep [process_name] can be used to search for specific processes.

Warnings

- ps does not provide real-time updates; use top or htop for continuous monitoring.

---

8. kill - Terminate a Process

What is kill

The kill command sends a signal to a process, typically used to terminate processes by specifying their process ID (PID).

Use Purpose

- **Terminate Processes**: Stop processes that are misbehaving or unresponsive.
- **Resource Management**: Free up system resources by ending unused processes.

Syntax

```
kill [PID]
```

Syntax Explanation

- **kill**: Command to send signals to processes.
    - ○ **[PID]**: The process ID to terminate.

Simple Code Example

```
kill 1234
```

Code Example Explanation

1. **Terminates** the process with PID 1234, freeing up resources.

Common Errors and Solutions

- **Error**: `kill: No such process`
  - **Solution**: Verify the PID of the target process.

Notes

- Use `kill -9` (SIGKILL) for forceful termination if `kill` alone does not work.

Warnings

- Be cautious with `kill -9`, as it forcefully ends processes without cleanup.

---

9. pkill - Terminate Processes by Name

What is pkill

The `pkill` command sends a signal to processes by name, allowing you to terminate multiple instances of the same process at once.

Use Purpose

- **Terminate Multiple Processes**: End all instances of a specific program.
- **Simplified Process Management**: Useful for terminating processes without specifying PIDs.

Syntax

```
pkill [process_name]
```

Syntax Explanation

- **pkill**: Command to terminate processes by name.
  - **[process_name]**: The name of the process to terminate.

Simple Code Example

```
pkill firefox
```

Code Example Explanation

1. **Terminates** all instances of `firefox`, closing all open browser windows.

Common Errors and Solutions
- **Error**: `pkill: No process found`
  - **Solution**: Ensure the process name is correct and that it is currently running.

Notes
- `pkill` is convenient when working with multiple instances of a process.

Warnings
- `pkill` may terminate all instances of a program, so use with care.

Chapter – 7 Networking & Internet

Chapter Overview

This chapter covers essential Linux commands for networking and internet tasks. These commands help users test connectivity, download files, transfer data, and troubleshoot network issues. Mastery of these commands is crucial for network administrators and users working with servers or remote connections.

Chapter Goal

- Learn commands for testing network connectivity and transferring files.
- Understand how to troubleshoot network issues by examining interfaces, routes, and DNS information.
- Gain skills for managing network connections and diagnosing connectivity problems.

Syntax Table

Serial No	Command	Syntax	Simple Example
1	Test Connectivity	`ping [options] [hostname/IP]`	`ping google.com`
2	Download Files	`wget [options] [URL]`	`wget http://example.com/file.zip`
3	Transfer Data	`curl [options] [URL]`	`curl http://example.com`
4	File Transfer	`ftp [hostname]`	`ftp ftp.example.com`
5	Display Network Interfaces	`ifconfig [options]`	`ifconfig`

6	Network Statistics	`netstat [options]`	`netstat -a`
7	Trace Network Route	`traceroute [hostname]`	`traceroute google.com`
8	Query DNS	`nslookup [hostname]`	`nslookup example.com`

Topic Explanations

1. ping - Test Connectivity to a Server

What is ping

The ping command tests connectivity to a specified host by sending Internet Control Message Protocol (ICMP) packets. It is commonly used to verify if a network connection is established between your device and the target server.

Use Purpose

- **Connectivity Testing**: Checks if a remote server or IP is reachable.
- **Network Latency**: Measures round-trip time (latency) between your system and the target.

Syntax

```
ping [options] [hostname/IP]
```

Syntax Explanation

- **ping**: Command to send ICMP packets.
    - **[options]**: Common options include:
        - **-c**: Specifies the number of packets to send (e.g., -c 4).
    - **[hostname/IP]**: The domain name or IP address to ping.

Simple Code Example

```
ping -c 4 google.com
```

Code Example Explanation

1. **Sends** 4 ICMP packets to google.com, measuring response times.

Common Errors and Solutions

- **Error**: `ping: unknown host`
  - **Solution**: Verify the hostname or check internet connectivity.

Notes

- A successful `ping` confirms the host is reachable, but firewall restrictions may block `ping` responses.

Warnings

- Continuous `ping` without limiting packets (`-c`) may cause network congestion.

---

2. wget - Download Files from the Internet

What is `wget`

The `wget` command downloads files from the internet via HTTP, HTTPS, or FTP protocols. It's often used for automating file downloads.

Use Purpose

- **File Download**: Retrieves files from URLs for offline use.
- **Automated Downloading**: Useful for batch file downloads in scripts.

Syntax

```
wget [options] [URL]
```

Syntax Explanation

- **wget**: Command to download files.
  - **[options]**: Customizes the download behavior, with common options including:
    - **-O**: Specifies output filename.
    - **-q**: Quiet mode, suppresses output.
  - **[URL]**: The web address of the file to download.

Simple Code Example

```
wget http://example.com/file.zip
```

Code Example Explanation

1. **Downloads** `file.zip` from `example.com` to the current directory.

Common Errors and Solutions
- **Error**: `wget: command not found`
    - **Solution**: Install wget using your package manager (e.g., `sudo apt install wget`).

Notes
- Use `-O` to rename downloaded files (e.g., `wget -O new_name.zip URL`).

Warnings
- Ensure the target URL is trustworthy to avoid downloading malicious files.

---

3. `curl` - Transfer Data to/from Servers

What is `curl`
The `curl` command transfers data to or from a server, supporting protocols like HTTP, FTP, and others. It's commonly used for making web requests or downloading web data.

Use Purpose
- **Download or Upload Files**: Transfers data using various internet protocols.
- **API Interactions**: Fetches or posts data to web APIs.

Syntax
```
curl [options] [URL]
```

Syntax Explanation
- **curl**: Command to transfer data.
    - **[options]**: Configures the data transfer:
        - `-o`: Saves the output to a file.
        - `-I`: Fetches headers only.
    - **[URL]**: The web address to send or retrieve data from.

Simple Code Example
```
curl -O http://example.com/file.zip
```

Code Example Explanation
1. **Downloads** `file.zip` from `example.com` and saves it in the current directory.

Common Errors and Solutions
- **Error**: `curl: (6) Could not resolve host`
  - **Solution**: Verify the URL and check internet connectivity.

Notes
- `curl` is versatile and supports complex web requests with headers, authentication, and more.

Warnings
- Avoid posting sensitive data without encryption (use HTTPS when possible).

---

4. `ftp` - Transfer Files Between Computers

What is `ftp`

The `ftp` command establishes a connection to a remote server for file transfer. It allows uploading and downloading of files between local and remote machines.

Use Purpose
- **File Transfer**: Upload and download files over FTP.
- **Remote File Management**: Manipulate files on a remote FTP server.

Syntax
```
ftp [hostname]
```

Syntax Explanation
- **ftp**: Command to initiate an FTP session.
  - **[hostname]**: The FTP server hostname or IP to connect to.

Simple Code Example
```
ftp ftp.example.com
```

Code Example Explanation
1. **Establishes** an FTP connection to `ftp.example.com`, prompting for login credentials.

Common Errors and Solutions
- **Error**: `ftp: connect: Connection refused`
  - **Solution**: Check FTP server status or firewall settings.

Notes
- For secure file transfer, consider using `sftp` or `scp`.

5. ifconfig - Display or Configure Network Interfaces

What is ifconfig

The ifconfig command displays and configures network interfaces. It provides details such as IP address, subnet mask, and MAC address for each network interface.

Use Purpose

- **Network Configuration**: View and configure network interface settings.
- **IP Address Verification**: Confirm local IP addresses for network troubleshooting.

Syntax

```
ifconfig [interface] [options]
```

Syntax Explanation

- **ifconfig**: Command to display or modify network interfaces.
    - **[interface]**: Specifies a network interface (e.g., eth0).
    - **[options]**: Additional configuration options, like up or down to enable/disable interfaces.

Simple Code Example

```
ifconfig
```

Code Example Explanation

1. **Displays** configuration information for all network interfaces.

Common Errors and Solutions

- **Error**: ifconfig: command not found
    - **Solution**: Use ip addr if ifconfig is unavailable or install the net-tools package.

Notes

- ifconfig is being phased out in favor of the ip command on newer systems.

Warnings

- Modifying network settings can disrupt connectivity; ensure correct configuration.

6. netstat - Network Statistics and Connections

What is netstat

The netstat command displays network statistics, including active connections, listening ports, and protocol usage.

Use Purpose

- **Monitor Network Connections**: View active connections and listening services.
- **Check Port Usage**: Identify open ports and associated processes.

Syntax

```
netstat [options]
```

Syntax Explanation

- **netstat**: Command to display network statistics.
    - ○ **[options]**: Common options include:
        - ■ **-a**: Shows all connections and listening ports.
        - ■ **-t**: Displays TCP connections.
        - ■ **-u**: Displays UDP connections.

Simple Code Example

```
netstat -a
```

Code Example Explanation

1. **Lists** all active connections and listening ports on the system.

Common Errors and Solutions

- **Error**: netstat: command not found
    - ○ **Solution**: Use ss on newer systems or install net-tools.

Notes

- netstat has been replaced by ss on many Linux distributions for network statistics.

Warnings

- Running netstat without sufficient permissions may restrict output details.

7. `traceroute` - Trace the Route Packets Take to a Network Host

What is `traceroute`

The `traceroute` command shows the path packets take from your system to a remote host. It displays each hop and the time taken for packets to reach each hop.

Use Purpose

- **Network Path Analysis**: Identify the path and delay of packets between your system and the target.
- **Troubleshoot Network Issues**: Detect network bottlenecks or unreachable segments.

Syntax

```
traceroute [hostname]
```

Syntax Explanation

- **traceroute**: Command to trace the network route.
    - ○ **[hostname]**: The domain name or IP address of the target host.

Simple Code Example

```
traceroute google.com
```

Code Example Explanation

1. **Displays** each hop along the path to `google.com`, showing the route and latency at each step.

Common Errors and Solutions

- **Error**: `traceroute: command not found`
    - ○ **Solution**: Install `traceroute` via your package manager.

Notes

- Firewalls may block traceroute packets, leading to incomplete results.

Warnings

- Excessive traceroute requests to a target may be considered suspicious activity.

8. nslookup - Query DNS Servers

What is nslookup

The nslookup command queries DNS servers to resolve domain names to IP addresses, or vice versa. It is useful for troubleshooting DNS issues.

Use Purpose

- **DNS Resolution**: Converts domain names to IP addresses and vice versa.
- **Troubleshoot DNS Issues**: Checks if DNS servers resolve domains correctly.

Syntax

```
nslookup [hostname]
```

Syntax Explanation

- **nslookup**: Command to query DNS records.
  - **[hostname]**: The domain name to resolve, or an IP address for reverse lookup.

Simple Code Example

```
nslookup example.com
```

Code Example Explanation

1. **Queries** DNS servers to resolve example.com to its IP address.

Common Errors and Solutions

- **Error**: nslookup: command not found
  - **Solution**: Install dnsutils or bind-utils package.

Notes

- nslookup is useful for identifying DNS issues or verifying domain configuration.

Warnings

- Use cautiously with unknown domains to avoid security risks.

Chapter – 8 Disk & Filesystem Management

Chapter Overview

This chapter covers essential Linux commands for managing disks, partitions, and filesystems. These commands allow users to create, format, mount, and compress files, enabling effective disk and data management. Mastery of these commands is crucial for system administrators responsible for disk organization and data handling.

Chapter Goal

- Learn how to partition disks, create filesystems, and manage mounts.
- Understand file compression and archiving commands for efficient data storage.
- Gain skills to manage disk space and handle large volumes of data.

Syntax Table

Seri al No	Command	Syntax	Simple Example
1	Partition Table Manipulation	`fdisk [device]`	`fdisk /dev/sda`
2	Partition Management	`parted [device]`	`parted /dev/sda`
3	Create a Filesystem	`mkfs [options] [device]`	`mkfs.ext4 /dev/sda1`
4	Mount a Filesystem	`mount [device] [directory]`	`mount /dev/sda1 /mnt`
5	Unmount a Filesystem	`umount [device/directory]`	`umount /mnt`

6	Archive Multiple Files	`tar [options] [archive_name] [files]`	`tar -cvf archive.tar /path/to/files`
7	Compress Files	`gzip [file]`	`gzip file.txt`
8	Decompress gzip Files	`gunzip [file]`	`gunzip file.txt.gz`
9	Compress Files (bzip2)	`bzip2 [file]`	`bzip2 file.txt`
10	Compress/Decompress ZIP Files	`zip/unzip [file.zip] [files]`	`zip archive.zip file1 file2`

Topic Explanations

1. fdisk - Partition Table Manipulation

What is fdisk

The `fdisk` command is used to manipulate disk partition tables. It allows you to create, modify, and delete partitions on a disk.

Use Purpose

- **Partition Management**: Modify partitions on a disk.
- **Disk Setup**: Prepare a disk for use by creating partition tables.

Syntax

```
fdisk [device]
```

Syntax Explanation

- **fdisk**: Command to open the partition table editor.
    - **[device]**: The disk device to partition (e.g., /dev/sda).

Simple Code Example

```
fdisk /dev/sda
```

Code Example Explanation

1. **Opens** the partition table editor for /dev/sda, allowing you to create, delete, or modify partitions.

Common Errors and Solutions

- **Error**: fdisk: cannot open /dev/sda: Permission denied
    - **Solution**: Run with sudo to ensure administrative privileges.

Notes

- fdisk supports only MBR partition tables; use parted for GPT.

Warnings

- Misuse of fdisk can lead to data loss. Ensure you understand partitioning before proceeding.

---

2. parted - Create and Manage Partitions

What is parted

The parted command is used to create and manage partitions on a disk, supporting both MBR and GPT partition tables.

Use Purpose

- **Partition Management**: Create and resize partitions.
- **Flexible Disk Setup**: Supports both MBR and GPT partitions.

Syntax

```
parted [device]
```

Syntax Explanation

- **parted**: Command to start the partition editor.
    - **[device]**: The disk to manage (e.g., /dev/sda).

Simple Code Example

```
parted /dev/sda
```

Code Example Explanation

1. **Launches** the partition editor for /dev/sda, enabling partition creation, deletion, and resizing.

Common Errors and Solutions

- **Error**: `parted: /dev/sda: unrecognised disk label`
  - ○ **Solution**: Use `mklabel` within `parted` to create a new partition table.

Notes

- `parted` is recommended for disks over 2 TB, as it supports GPT.

Warnings

- Changing partitions on a disk may result in data loss if not handled carefully.

---

3. `mkfs` - Create a Filesystem on a Device

What is `mkfs`

The `mkfs` (make filesystem) command formats a partition, creating a new filesystem on it.

Use Purpose

- **Create Filesystem**: Prepares a partition for data storage.
- **Specify Filesystem Type**: Supports various filesystems like `ext4`, `xfs`, `vfat`.

Syntax

```
mkfs [options] [device]
```

Syntax Explanation

- **mkfs**: Command to create a filesystem.
  - ○ **[options]**: Specifies the filesystem type (e.g., `-t ext4`).
  - ○ **[device]**: The partition to format (e.g., `/dev/sda1`).

Simple Code Example

```
mkfs.ext4 /dev/sda1
```

Code Example Explanation

1. **Formats** the `/dev/sda1` partition with the `ext4` filesystem, preparing it for use.

Common Errors and Solutions

- **Error**: `mkfs.ext4: Permission denied`
  - ○ **Solution**: Use `sudo` for administrative access.

Notes

- Use `mkfs -t [type]` to specify the filesystem type (e.g., `mkfs -t vfat` for FAT).

Warnings

- Running `mkfs` will erase all data on the partition; double-check the device before proceeding.

---

4. mount - Mount a Filesystem

What is mount

The `mount` command attaches a filesystem to a specified directory, making it accessible.

Use Purpose

- **Attach Filesystems**: Mounts a device to a directory for access.
- **Temporary Storage Access**: Temporarily mounts devices like USBs.

Syntax

```
mount [device] [directory]
```

Syntax Explanation

- **mount**: Command to attach a filesystem.
    - **[device]**: The device or partition to mount (e.g., `/dev/sda1`).
    - **[directory]**: The directory to mount to (e.g., `/mnt`).

Simple Code Example

```
mount /dev/sda1 /mnt
```

Code Example Explanation

1. **Mounts** the `/dev/sda1` partition to the `/mnt` directory, making its files accessible at `/mnt`.

Common Errors and Solutions

- **Error**: `mount: only root can do that`
    - **Solution**: Run `sudo mount` for administrative privileges.

Notes

- Check `/etc/fstab` for persistent mounts that load on boot.

5. umount - Unmount a Filesystem

What is umount

The umount command detaches a mounted filesystem, ensuring data integrity before device removal.

Use Purpose

- **Detach Filesystems**: Safely unmounts devices.
- **Prevent Data Loss**: Ensures all data is written before removal.

Syntax

```
umount [device/directory]
```

Syntax Explanation

- **umount**: Command to unmount a filesystem.
    - **[device/directory]**: Specifies the device or mount point to unmount.

Simple Code Example

```
umount /mnt
```

Code Example Explanation

1. **Unmounts** the filesystem mounted at /mnt, safely detaching the device.

Common Errors and Solutions

- **Error**: umount: target is busy
    - **Solution**: Close open files and use lsof to identify processes using the mount.

Notes

- Always unmount USB drives and external storage to prevent data corruption.

Warnings

- Force unmounting with -l may lead to data loss; use with caution.

---

6. tar - Archive Multiple Files

What is tar

The tar command bundles multiple files into a single archive file, preserving directory structure and file permissions.

Use Purpose
- **File Archiving**: Groups multiple files for easier handling.
- **Backup Creation**: Creates compressed backups with optional compression.

Syntax
```
tar [options] [archive_name] [files]
```

Syntax Explanation
- **tar**: Command to create or extract archives.
  - **[options]**: Common options include:
    - **-c**: Creates a new archive.
    - **-v**: Verbose, shows file names.
    - **-f**: Specifies archive filename.
  - **[archive_name]**: Name of the output archive (e.g., backup.tar).
  - **[files]**: Files or directories to include in the archive.

Simple Code Example
```
tar -cvf archive.tar /path/to/files
```

Code Example Explanation
1. **Creates** an archive named archive.tar containing the files in /path/to/files.

Common Errors and Solutions
- **Error**: tar: Permission denied
  - **Solution**: Run with sudo or check directory permissions.

Notes
- Use -z to compress with gzip, creating .tar.gz archives.

Warnings
- Be careful with paths to avoid including unintended files in the archive.

---

7. gzip - Compress Files

What is gzip
The gzip command compresses files using the gzip compression algorithm, reducing file sizes.

Use Purpose

- **File Compression**: Reduces file sizes for storage or transfer.
- **Space Management**: Frees up disk space by compressing files.

Syntax

```
gzip [file]
```

Syntax Explanation

- **gzip**: Command to compress files.
  - **[file]**: Specifies the file to compress (e.g., file.txt).

Simple Code Example

```
gzip file.txt
```

Code Example Explanation

1. **Compresses** file.txt, resulting in file.txt.gz.

Common Errors and Solutions

- **Error**: gzip: file.txt.gz already exists
  - **Solution**: Use -f to force overwrite if needed.

Notes

- gzip deletes the original file by default after compression.

Warnings

- Decompress files with gunzip if you need to restore the original format.

---

8. gunzip - Decompress gzip Files

What is gunzip

The gunzip command decompresses files compressed with gzip, restoring them to their original format.

Use Purpose

- **File Decompression**: Restores compressed files for use.
- **Space Recovery**: Expands compressed files back to original form.

Syntax

```
gunzip [file]
```

Syntax Explanation

- **gunzip**: Command to decompress gzip files.

- [file]: Specifies the .gz file to decompress (e.g., `file.txt.gz`).

Simple Code Example

```
gunzip file.txt.gz
```

Code Example Explanation

1. **Decompresses** `file.txt.gz`, restoring it to `file.txt`.

Common Errors and Solutions

- **Error**: `gunzip: file.txt already exists`
    - **Solution**: Use `-f` to overwrite existing files if needed.

Notes

- Use `gzip -d` as an alternative to decompress files.

Warnings

- Ensure sufficient disk space is available for decompression.

---

9. bzip2 - Compress Files Using the bzip2 Algorithm

What is bzip2

The `bzip2` command compresses files using the `bzip2` algorithm, achieving high compression ratios.

Use Purpose

- **Enhanced Compression**: Compresses files with higher efficiency than gzip.
- **Space Management**: Reduces file sizes for storage or transfer.

Syntax

```
bzip2 [file]
```

Syntax Explanation

- **bzip2**: Command to compress files.
    - **[file]**: Specifies the file to compress (e.g., `file.txt`).

Simple Code Example

```
bzip2 file.txt
```

Code Example Explanation

1. **Compresses** `file.txt`, resulting in `file.txt.bz2`.

Common Errors and Solutions

- **Error**: `bzip2: file.txt.bz2 already exists`

       ○ **Solution**: Use `-f` to force overwrite if needed.

Notes

- Use `bunzip2` to decompress `.bz2` files.

Warnings

- bzip2 compresses slowly but results in smaller file sizes.

---

10. `zip/unzip` - Compress and Decompress ZIP Files

What is `zip/unzip`

The `zip` command compresses files into ZIP format, and `unzip` decompresses ZIP files. ZIP format is widely used for cross-platform compatibility.

Use Purpose

- **Cross-Platform Compression**: ZIP files are compatible with most operating systems.
- **Easy File Management**: Bundles multiple files and directories into one compressed file.

Syntax

```
zip [options] [archive.zip] [files]
unzip [options] [archive.zip]
```

Syntax Explanation

- **zip**: Command to compress files into a ZIP archive.
    - ○ **[options]**: Common options include:
        - ■ **-r**: Recursively add files in a directory.
    - ○ **[archive.zip]**: Name of the output ZIP file.
    - ○ **[files]**: Files or directories to compress.
- **unzip**: Command to decompress ZIP files.

Simple Code Example

```
zip archive.zip file1 file2
unzip archive.zip
```

Code Example Explanation

1. **Creates** `archive.zip` containing `file1` and `file2`.
2. **Extracts** `archive.zip`, restoring `file1` and `file2`.

Chapter – 9 Permissions & Ownership

Chapter Overview

This chapter covers essential Linux commands for managing file permissions, ownership, and user and group accounts. These commands allow users to control access to files, set default permissions, and manage user accounts and passwords. Understanding permissions and ownership is crucial for system security and effective access management.

Chapter Goal

- Learn to set file permissions and manage file ownership.
- Understand how to create, modify, and delete user and group accounts.
- Gain skills to ensure secure and organized access to files and resources.

Syntax Table

Serial No	Command	Syntax	Simple Example
1	Change File Permissions	`chmod [options] mode [file]`	`chmod 755 file.txt`
2	Change File Owner	`chown [options] owner[:group] [file]`	`chown user1 file.txt`
3	Set Default Permissions	`umask [mode]`	`umask 022`
4	Create a New User	`useradd [options] username`	`useradd newuser`
5	Modify a User Account	`usermod [options] username`	`usermod -aG sudo newuser`

6	Delete a User Account	`userdel [options] username`	`userdel newuser`
7	Create a New Group	`groupadd [options] groupname`	`groupadd developers`
8	Update User Passwords	`passwd [options] username`	`passwd newuser`

Topic Explanations

1. chmod - Change File Permissions

What is chmod

The chmod command modifies file or directory permissions, allowing the owner, group, or others to read, write, or execute the file.

Use Purpose

- **Access Control**: Sets who can read, write, or execute a file.
- **Secure File Management**: Limits unauthorized access to sensitive files.

Syntax

```
chmod [options] mode [file]
```

Syntax Explanation

- **chmod**: Command to change file permissions.
  - ○ **[options]**: Common options include:
    - ■ **-R**: Recursively changes permissions of files in directories.
  - ○ **mode**: The permissions to set, specified as octal (e.g., 755) or symbolic notation (e.g., u+rwx).
  - ○ **[file]**: Specifies the file or directory to modify.

Simple Code Example

```
chmod 755 file.txt
```

Code Example Explanation

1. **Sets permissions** on file.txt so the owner can read, write, and execute (7), while group and others can read and execute (5).

Common Errors and Solutions
- **Error**: chmod: Permission denied
    - **Solution**: Run with sudo if required for files owned by other users.

Notes
- Octal notation: 4 for read, 2 for write, 1 for execute, combined for each permission level.

Warnings
- Be cautious with write permissions for others to prevent unauthorized modifications.

---

2. chown - Change File Owner

What is chown
The chown command changes the owner or group of a file or directory, allowing file ownership to be transferred between users.

Use Purpose
- **Ownership Management**: Assigns ownership of files to specific users or groups.
- **Security**: Helps control access to files by managing file ownership.

Syntax
```
chown [options] owner[:group] [file]
```

Syntax Explanation
- **chown**: Command to change file owner.
    - **[options]**: Common options include:
        - **-R**: Recursively changes ownership in directories.
    - **owner[**
      ]: Specifies the new owner and optionally the group.
    - **[file]**: The file or directory to change ownership of.

Simple Code Example
```
chown user1 file.txt
```

Code Example Explanation
1. **Changes the ownership** of file.txt to user1.

Common Errors and Solutions

- **Error**: chown: Permission denied
    - **Solution**: Use sudo for administrative privileges.

Notes

- To change only the group, use chown :groupname file.

Warnings

- Misuse may lead to unintended access restrictions.

---

3. umask - Set Default Permissions

What is umask

The umask command sets the default permissions for new files and directories, determining which permissions are withheld by default.

Use Purpose

- **Default Permissions**: Controls default permissions for newly created files and directories.
- **Secure Defaults**: Ensures files are not created with overly permissive settings.

Syntax

```
umask [mode]
```

Syntax Explanation

- **umask**: Command to set default permissions.
    - **mode**: The permissions to withhold, specified as an octal value (e.g., 022).

Simple Code Example

```
umask 022
```

Code Example Explanation

1. **Sets the default permission** mask so that new files have 755 permissions by default.

Common Errors and Solutions

- **Error**: Misinterpreting octal values can lead to incorrect default permissions.
    - **Solution**: Use umask -S to check symbolic notation.

Notes

- Common umask values: 022 (755 for directories) and 027 (750 for directories).

Warnings

- Misconfigured umask can result in overly permissive or restrictive defaults.

4. useradd - Create a New User

What is useradd

The useradd command creates a new user account, adding the user to the system with default or specified options.

Use Purpose

- **User Account Creation**: Adds new users to the system.
- **Access Management**: Controls user access and permissions by creating accounts.

Syntax

```
useradd [options] username
```

Syntax Explanation

- **useradd**: Command to add new users.
    - **[options]**: Common options include:
        - **-m**: Creates a home directory for the user.
        - **-G**: Adds the user to supplementary groups.
    - **username**: The name of the new user account.

Simple Code Example

```
useradd -m newuser
```

Code Example Explanation

1. **Creates a new user** newuser with a home directory.

Common Errors and Solutions

- **Error**: useradd: Permission denied
    - **Solution**: Run with sudo for administrative access.

Notes

- Always set a password for new users with passwd.

Warnings

- Avoid adding users to sensitive groups without a valid reason.

5. usermod - Modify a User Account

What is usermod

The usermod command modifies an existing user account, allowing changes to username, group memberships, and more.

Use Purpose

- **Account Management**: Updates user account settings.
- **Flexible Access Control**: Adds users to groups or changes account properties.

Syntax

```
usermod [options] username
```

Syntax Explanation

- **usermod**: Command to modify user accounts.
  - ○ **[options]**: Common options include:
    - ■ **-aG**: Adds user to a group without removing existing memberships.
  - ○ **username**: The name of the user account to modify.

Simple Code Example

```
usermod -aG sudo newuser
```

Code Example Explanation

1. **Adds newuser to the sudo group**, granting administrative privileges.

Common Errors and Solutions

- **Error**: usermod: Permission denied
  - ○ **Solution**: Run with sudo for administrative access.

Notes

- Use -aG carefully; omitting -a can replace all group memberships.

Warnings

- Adding users to sensitive groups can expose the system to security risks.

---

6. userdel - Delete a User Account

What is userdel

The userdel command removes a user account from the system, optionally deleting the user's home directory.

Use Purpose
- **Account Removal**: Deletes users who no longer need access.
- **Resource Management**: Frees up system resources by removing inactive accounts.

Syntax
```
userdel [options] username
```

Syntax Explanation
- **userdel**: Command to delete user accounts.
  - **[options]**: Common options include:
    - **-r**: Removes the user's home directory.
  - **username**: The name of the user account to delete.

Simple Code Example
```
userdel -r newuser
```

Code Example Explanation
1. **Deletes newuser** and their home directory.

Common Errors and Solutions
- **Error**: userdel: Permission denied
  - **Solution**: Run with sudo for administrative privileges.

Notes
- User files outside the home directory are not deleted.

Warnings
- Deleting users without -r leaves their home directory intact.

---

7. groupadd - Create a New Group
What is groupadd
The groupadd command creates a new group, allowing users to share permissions based on group membership.

Use Purpose
- **Group Creation**: Creates groups to manage access control for multiple users.
- **Permission Management**: Allows group-based access to files and resources.

Syntax
```
groupadd [options] groupname
```

Syntax Explanation
- **groupadd**: Command to create groups.

○ **[options]**: Common options include specifying group ID (-g).

○ **groupname**: The name of the new group.

Simple Code Example

```
groupadd developers
```

Code Example Explanation

1. **Creates** a group named `developers` for assigning group permissions.

Common Errors and Solutions

- **Error**: `groupadd: Permission denied`

  ○ **Solution**: Run with `sudo` for administrative access.

Notes

- Assign users to the group with `usermod -aG`.

Warnings

- Avoid group name duplication, which may cause conflicts.

---

8. passwd - Update User Passwords

What is passwd

The `passwd` command updates a user's password, ensuring secure access to user accounts.

Use Purpose

- **Password Management**: Allows users and admins to set or update passwords.
- **Account Security**: Ensures accounts are protected with passwords.

Syntax

```
passwd [options] username
```

Syntax Explanation

- **passwd**: Command to change passwords.
  ○ **[options]**: Common options include:
    ■ **-e**: Forces password expiration.
  ○ **username**: Specifies the account to update (optional for the current user).

Simple Code Example

```
passwd newuser
```

Code Example Explanation
1. **Prompts for a new password** for `newuser`.

Common Errors and Solutions
- **Error**: `passwd: Permission denied`
    - ○ **Solution**: Use `sudo` when updating another user's password.

Notes
- Regularly updating passwords enhances security.

Warnings
- Avoid setting weak passwords to maintain account security.

Chapter – 10 Software & Package Management

Chapter Overview

This chapter introduces essential commands for managing software packages on Linux systems, focusing on Debian/Ubuntu-based systems and RHEL/CentOS-based systems. These commands allow users to install, update, and remove software packages, making system management and software deployment efficient.

Chapter Goal

- Learn to install, update, and manage software packages on both Debian/Ubuntu and RHEL/CentOS systems.
- Understand how to troubleshoot package installation issues and manage repositories.
- Gain skills for maintaining a clean and up-to-date Linux system.

Syntax Table

Serial No	Command	Syntax	Simple Example

1	Advanced Package Tool (apt)	`apt [options] [command] [package]`	`apt install nginx`
2	Package Handling Utility	`apt-get [options] [command] [package]`	`apt-get update`
3	Package Management (yum)	`yum [options] [command] [package]`	`yum install httpd`
4	Next-Generation Package Mgmt	`dnf [options] [command] [package]`	`dnf install httpd`

Topic Explanations

1. apt - Advanced Package Tool

What is apt

The apt command is a high-level package management tool used on Debian-based distributions like Ubuntu. It simplifies the process of installing, updating, and removing software packages, automatically managing dependencies.

Use Purpose

- **Install Software**: Easily installs software from official repositories.
- **System Updates**: Keeps the system software up-to-date.
- **Dependency Management**: Ensures required packages are installed.

Syntax

```
apt [options] [command] [package]
```

Syntax Explanation

- **apt**: High-level package management tool.
  - **[options]**: Common options include:
    - **-y**: Automatically answer "yes" to prompts.

- ○ **[command]**: Specifies the action, such as `install`, `update`, or `remove`.
- ○ **[package]**: The package name to install, update, or remove.

Simple Code Example

```
apt install nginx
```

Code Example Explanation

1. **Installs** the `nginx` web server package, handling dependencies and downloading files.

Common Errors and Solutions

- **Error**: `E: Unable to locate package`
  - ○ **Solution**: Run `apt update` to refresh the package list.

Notes

- Use `apt update` to fetch the latest package lists before installation.

Warnings

- Be cautious with `apt remove` as it may uninstall essential packages.

2. apt-get - Package Handling Utility

What is apt-get

The `apt-get` command is a lower-level tool for package management on Debian-based systems. It provides more granular control over package handling but requires specific commands for each action.

Use Purpose

- **Package Management**: Manages the installation, removal, and update of packages.
- **Scripted Use**: Often used in scripts for automated package management tasks.

Syntax

```
apt-get [options] [command] [package]
```

Syntax Explanation

- **apt-get**: Command for package management.

- [options]: Configures behavior (e.g., -y for automatic yes).
- [command]: Actions include `install`, `remove`, `update`, `upgrade`.
- [package]: The package name, when applicable.

Simple Code Example

```
apt-get update
```

Code Example Explanation

1. **Updates** the list of available packages, ensuring access to the latest software versions.

Common Errors and Solutions

- **Error**: `E: Could not get lock /var/lib/dpkg/lock`
  - **Solution**: Ensure no other package management process is running.

Notes

- `apt-get` is compatible with older systems; `apt` is a newer alternative for most tasks.

Warnings

- Avoid interrupting `apt-get upgrade` to prevent package corruption.

---

3. yum - Install, Remove, and Update Packages

What is yum

The yum (Yellowdog Updater, Modified) command is a package management tool for RHEL-based systems like CentOS and Fedora. It simplifies package installation, updates, and dependency management.

Use Purpose

- **Software Installation**: Installs software packages with dependency handling.
- **System Updates**: Keeps the system packages up-to-date.
- **Repository Management**: Manages packages from configured repositories.

Syntax

```
yum [options] [command] [package]
```

Syntax Explanation
- **yum**: Command for managing packages.
  - ○ **[options]**: Common options include:
    - ■ **-y**: Automatically answer "yes" to prompts.
  - ○ **[command]**: Specifies the action, such as `install`, `update`, or `remove`.
  - ○ **[package]**: The name of the package for installation, removal, or update.

Simple Code Example
```
yum install httpd
```

Code Example Explanation
1. **Installs** the `httpd` (Apache web server) package, handling dependencies and downloading necessary files.

Common Errors and Solutions
- **Error**: `yum: command not found`
  - ○ **Solution**: Use `dnf` on newer RHEL-based systems like Fedora 22+ and CentOS 8+.

Notes
- Use `yum update` regularly to keep packages updated.

Warnings
- Be cautious with `yum remove`, as it may uninstall important dependencies.

---

4. dnf - Next-Generation Package Management (CentOS/RHEL)

What is dnf
The `dnf` (Dandified YUM) command is an advanced package management tool that replaces `yum` on newer RHEL-based systems like CentOS 8 and Fedora. It has improved dependency resolution and better handling of software packages.

Use Purpose
- **Modern Package Management**: Simplifies software management with enhanced features.

- **Install, Update, and Remove Software**: Manages software packages with fewer issues than yum.
- **Efficient Dependency Handling**: Improves upon yum with faster dependency resolution.

Syntax

```
dnf [options] [command] [package]
```

Syntax Explanation

- **dnf**: Command for next-generation package management.
  - **[options]**: Common options include:
    - **-y**: Automatically answer "yes" to prompts.
  - **[command]**: Actions include install, update, remove, list.
  - **[package]**: The package name to manage.

Simple Code Example

```
dnf install httpd
```

Code Example Explanation

1. **Installs** the httpd (Apache web server) package, automatically resolving dependencies and downloading necessary files.

Common Errors and Solutions

- **Error**: dnf: command not found
  - **Solution**: Ensure you're on a system that supports dnf, such as CentOS 8 or Fedora.

Notes

- dnf provides a more user-friendly output and better performance than yum.

Warnings

- Use caution when using dnf remove to avoid uninstalling critical packages.

Chapter – 11 Scheduling & Automation

Chapter Overview

This chapter covers essential Linux commands for scheduling tasks and managing system services. With these commands, users can automate recurring tasks, schedule one-time jobs, and manage services to ensure that the system runs efficiently and reliably. Automation and service management are key skills for system administrators and anyone responsible for maintaining a Linux environment.

Chapter Goal

- Learn to schedule recurring and one-time tasks using `cron`, `crontab`, and `at`.
- Understand how to start, stop, and manage system services with `systemctl` and `service`.
- Gain skills to view and analyze system logs with `journalctl`.

Syntax Table

Serial No	Command	Syntax	Simple Example
1	Schedule Recurring Tasks	`cron` (used via `crontab`)	(N/A – runs scheduled tasks)
2	Edit Cron Jobs Table	`crontab -e`	`crontab -e`
3	Schedule One-Time Task	`at [time]`	`echo "command"`
4	Manage Services	`systemctl [command] [service]`	`systemctl start apache2`

5	Start/Stop Services	`service [service] [command]`	`service apache2 restart`
6	View Logs	`journalctl [options]`	`journalctl -u apache2`

Topic Explanations

1. cron - Schedule Tasks to Run at Specific Intervals

What is cron

The cron daemon runs scheduled tasks at specified intervals. It is commonly used for automating repetitive tasks like backups, maintenance scripts, and updates.

Use Purpose

- **Automate Recurring Tasks**: Schedules regular tasks for system maintenance.
- **Unattended Execution**: Runs jobs without requiring user interaction.

Syntax

```
cron (runs as a daemon)
```

Syntax Explanation

- **cron**: A background service that executes commands according to the schedules set in crontab.

Simple Code Example

```
# Use `crontab -e` to add the following line
0 2 * * * /usr/bin/backup.sh
```

Code Example Explanation

1. **Schedules** the backup.sh script to run daily at 2:00 AM.

Common Errors and Solutions

- **Error**: cron: no crontab for user
  - **Solution**: Use crontab -e to create one.

Notes

- Use crontab -l to list current cron jobs.

2. crontab - Edit the Cron Jobs Table

What is crontab

The crontab command is used to create, edit, list, or delete cron jobs, specifying tasks and their schedules for the cron daemon.

Use Purpose

- **Edit Scheduled Tasks**: Adds or modifies scheduled jobs for automation.
- **View Scheduled Jobs**: Lists currently active jobs for a user.

Syntax

```
crontab [options]
```

Syntax Explanation

- **crontab**: Command to edit cron jobs.
  - **[options]**:
    - **-e**: Opens the cron table for editing.
    - **-l**: Lists the current cron jobs.

Simple Code Example

```
crontab -e
```

Code Example Explanation

1. **Opens** the cron table in the default editor, allowing the user to add or modify cron jobs.

Common Errors and Solutions

- **Error**: crontab: command not found
  - **Solution**: Ensure cron is installed and running.

Notes

- Crontab entries follow the format: minute hour day month day_of_week command.

Warnings

- Incorrect syntax in crontab can prevent jobs from running.

3. at - Schedule a Task to Run Once at a Particular Time

What is at

The at command schedules a one-time task to run at a specified time, which can be useful for delayed or timed tasks.

Use Purpose
- **One-Time Scheduling**: Schedules tasks that should run once at a specified time.
- **Flexible Timing**: Allows scheduling with relative terms like `now + 1 hour`.

Syntax
```
at [time]
```

Syntax Explanation
- **at**: Command to schedule a one-time task.
  - **[time]**: Specifies when the task should run (e.g., `now + 5 minutes` or `10:00`).

Simple Code Example
```
echo "reboot" | at 03:00
```

Code Example Explanation
1. **Schedules** a system reboot at 3:00 AM.

Common Errors and Solutions
- **Error**: `at: command not found`
  - **Solution**: Install `at` using the package manager.

Notes
- Use `atq` to view pending tasks and `atrm` to remove scheduled tasks.

Warnings
- `at` tasks are deleted after execution; use `cron` for recurring tasks.

---

4. systemctl - Start, Stop, and Manage Services
What is systemctl
The `systemctl` command manages services and units on systems that use `systemd`, controlling starting, stopping, enabling, or disabling services.

Use Purpose
- **Service Management**: Manages services to ensure they start, stop, or restart as needed.
- **System Stability**: Ensures critical services remain active and responsive.

Syntax

```
systemctl [command] [service]
```

Syntax Explanation

- **systemctl**: Command to manage services.
  - **[command]**: Common commands include:
    - **start**: Starts the service.
    - **stop**: Stops the service.
    - **restart**: Restarts the service.
    - **enable**: Enables the service to start on boot.
    - **disable**: Disables the service from starting on boot.
  - **[service]**: The name of the service (e.g., apache2 or nginx).

Simple Code Example

```
systemctl start apache2
```

Code Example Explanation

1. **Starts** the apache2 (Apache web server) service.

Common Errors and Solutions

- **Error**: Failed to start apache2.service: Unit apache2.service not found
  - **Solution**: Verify the service name or install the required service.

Notes

- Use systemctl status [service] to check the service status.

Warnings

- Stopping critical services like networking can disrupt system operation.

---

5. service - Start, Stop, and Restart System Services

What is service

The service command manages services on Linux systems, providing a simplified interface for starting, stopping, and restarting services.

Use Purpose

- **Simplified Service Management**: Easily controls services without needing full `systemctl` commands.
- **Legacy Systems**: Often available on older systems or as a compatibility layer.

Syntax

```
service [service] [command]
```

Syntax Explanation

- **service**: Command to manage services.
  - **[service]**: The name of the service (e.g., `apache2` or `nginx`).
  - **[command]**: Commands like `start`, `stop`, `restart`, and `status`.

Simple Code Example

```
service apache2 restart
```

Code Example Explanation

1. **Restarts** the apache2 service, applying any recent changes.

Common Errors and Solutions

- **Error**: `service: command not found`
  - **Solution**: Use `systemctl` if `service` is unavailable.

Notes

- `service` is commonly used for backward compatibility with `sysvinit` systems.

Warnings

- Some distributions are moving entirely to `systemctl`; `service` may be deprecated.

6. `journalctl` - View Logs Generated by systemd

What is `journalctl`

The `journalctl` command views logs generated by `systemd`. It is useful for analyzing service output, troubleshooting issues, and reviewing historical system data.

Use Purpose

- **Log Analysis**: Provides a comprehensive view of system logs.
- **Troubleshooting**: Assists in diagnosing and resolving service issues.

Syntax

```
journalctl [options]
```

Syntax Explanation

- **journalctl**: Command to view system logs.
  - **[options]**:
    - **-u [service]**: Filters logs for a specific service.
    - **-b**: Shows logs since the last system boot.
    - **--since**: Filters logs from a specific date or time.

Simple Code Example

```
journalctl -u apache2
```

Code Example Explanation

1. **Displays** logs for the apache2 service, useful for troubleshooting and monitoring.

Common Errors and Solutions

- **Error**: No journal files were found
  - **Solution**: Ensure systemd-journald service is running and that logging is enabled.

Notes

- Use `journalctl -xe` for detailed logs, especially for recent service errors.

Warnings

- Reviewing logs extensively may require elevated privileges (e.g., `sudo`).

Chapter – 12 Development Tools

Chapter Overview

This chapter covers essential Linux tools for software development, including code compilation, debugging, and version control. These tools are fundamental for compiling source code, automating builds, debugging programs, and managing code changes across versions. Mastering these commands helps developers efficiently manage and troubleshoot code, enabling smooth and productive development workflows.

Chapter Goal

- Learn to compile, build, and debug programs using tools like gcc, make, gdb, and ldd.
- Understand how to manage and track code changes with version control systems like git and svn.
- Gain skills to troubleshoot dependencies, automate builds, and manage source code versions effectively.

Syntax Table

Seria l No	Command	Syntax	Simple Example
1	GNU Compiler Collection	gcc [options] [source_file]	gcc -o program program.c
2	Build Automation	make [options] [target]	make
3	Debugging Programs	gdb [program]	gdb ./program
4	Print Dependencies	ldd [options] [program]	ldd ./program

5	Version Control System	`git [command] [options]`	`git clone https://repo_ur l.git`
6	Apache Subversion	`svn [command] [options]`	`svn checkout https://repo_ur l`

Topic Explanations

1. gcc - GNU Compiler Collection

What is gcc

The gcc command is part of the GNU Compiler Collection and is used to compile C, C++, and other language source code files into executable binaries. It is one of the most widely used compilers in Linux environments.

Use Purpose

- **Code Compilation**: Transforms source code into machine-executable binaries.
- **Error Checking**: Provides warnings and errors to help improve code quality.

Syntax

```
gcc [options] [source_file]
```

Syntax Explanation

- **gcc**: Command for compiling source code.
    - **[options]**: Configures compilation settings, such as:
        - **-o [output_file]**: Specifies the output file name.
        - **-Wall**: Enables common warnings.
    - **[source_file]**: The source code file to compile (e.g., `program.c`).

Simple Code Example

```
gcc -o program program.c
```

Code Example Explanation

1. **Compiles** `program.c` into an executable named `program`, producing an optimized binary.

Common Errors and Solutions

- **Error**: `gcc: command not found`
    - **Solution**: Install gcc using the package manager (e.g., `sudo apt install gcc`).

Notes

- Use gcc `-g` to include debugging information for use with gdb.

Warnings

- Always address warnings shown during compilation to improve code quality.

2. make - Build Automation Tool for Compiling Code

What is make

The make command is a build automation tool that reads a file called `Makefile` to determine how to compile and link a program. It simplifies complex build processes by managing dependencies.

Use Purpose

- **Automated Builds**: Compiles projects with multiple source files based on instructions in a `Makefile`.
- **Dependency Management**: Recompiles only updated files, saving time.

Syntax

```
make [options] [target]
```

Syntax Explanation

- **make**: Command to automate builds.
    - **[options]**: Configures the behavior, such as `-f` to specify an alternative `Makefile`.
    - **[target]**: Specifies the build target defined in the `Makefile` (e.g., `clean`, `all`).

Simple Code Example

```
make
```

Code Example Explanation
1. **Builds** the default target specified in the `Makefile`, usually compiling the program.

Common Errors and Solutions
- **Error**: `make: No targets specified and no makefile found`
    - **Solution**: Ensure a `Makefile` exists in the directory.

Notes
- `Makefile` syntax defines dependencies and rules, allowing efficient project builds.

Warnings
- Improper `Makefile` syntax can cause unexpected build errors or incomplete builds.

---

3. gdb - GNU Debugger
What is gdb
The gdb (GNU Debugger) is a tool that allows developers to debug programs by setting breakpoints, examining memory and variables, and stepping through code execution.

Use Purpose
- **Debugging Programs**: Identifies issues by stepping through code execution.
- **Error Analysis**: Examines variables, memory, and program flow to locate bugs.

Syntax
```
gdb [program]
```
Syntax Explanation
- **gdb**: Command to start the debugger.
    - **[program]**: The compiled executable to debug (e.g., `./program`).

Simple Code Example
```
gdb ./program
```
Code Example Explanation
1. **Launches** gdb with the `program` executable, allowing debugging commands to be entered.

Common Errors and Solutions
- **Error**: gdb: command not found
  - **Solution**: Install gdb using the package manager.

Notes
- Use gcc -g when compiling to include debugging information in the binary.

Warnings
- Avoid debugging production binaries to prevent unintended system modifications.

---

4. ldd - Print Shared Object Dependencies

What is ldd

The ldd command lists the shared libraries required by a given executable. It is useful for identifying dependencies and troubleshooting missing libraries.

Use Purpose
- **Dependency Checking**: Identifies shared libraries required by an executable.
- **Troubleshooting**: Helps locate missing dependencies that may cause runtime errors.

Syntax

```
ldd [options] [program]
```

Syntax Explanation
- **ldd**: Command to list dependencies.
  - **[options]**: Configures the behavior (rarely used).
  - **[program]**: The program or library file to check (e.g., ./program).

Simple Code Example

```
ldd ./program
```

Code Example Explanation
1. **Lists** shared library dependencies for program, indicating if any dependencies are missing.

Common Errors and Solutions
- **Error**: not a dynamic executable
  - **Solution**: Ensure you are analyzing a dynamically linked executable.

Notes
- `ldd` output includes the paths of linked libraries, helpful for verifying dependencies.

Warnings
- Only use `ldd` on trusted binaries, as it may execute code during analysis.

---

5. `git` - Distributed Version Control System

What is `git`

The `git` command is a version control system that tracks changes in source code, enabling multiple developers to collaborate, manage branches, and maintain a history of changes.

Use Purpose
- **Version Control**: Manages code changes over time and across contributors.
- **Collaboration**: Enables teams to work on code simultaneously with branch management.

Syntax

```
git [command] [options]
```

Syntax Explanation
- **git**: Command to interact with the version control system.
  - **[command]**: Specifies the action, such as `clone`, `commit`, or `push`.
  - **[options]**: Modifies behavior, like -m to add a commit message.

Simple Code Example

```
git clone https://repo_url.git
```

Code Example Explanation
1. **Clones** a remote repository into a local directory, creating a copy of the code.

Common Errors and Solutions
- **Error**: `fatal: repository not found`
  - **Solution**: Verify the repository URL and permissions.

Notes

- Use `git status` to check the status of your local repository.

Warnings

- Regularly commit changes to avoid losing work when switching branches.

---

6. svn - Apache Subversion for Version Control

What is svn

The `svn` (Subversion) command is a version control system that manages code changes and collaboration. It uses a central repository model, contrasting with `git`'s distributed model.

Use Purpose

- **Centralized Version Control**: Manages code changes in a central repository.
- **Collaboration**: Enables teams to work on code with check-in/check-out processes.

Syntax

```
svn [command] [options]
```

Syntax Explanation

- **svn**: Command to interact with the version control system.
    - ○ **[command]**: Specifies the action, such as `checkout`, `commit`, or `update`.
    - ○ **[options]**: Additional options to modify behavior.

Simple Code Example

```
svn checkout https://repo_url
```

Code Example Explanation

1. **Creates a local copy** of the repository at the specified URL, allowing for further changes and commits.

Common Errors and Solutions

- **Error**: `svn: E170013: Unable to connect to a repository`
    - ○ **Solution**: Check the repository URL and network connection.

Notes

- Subversion supports atomic commits, reducing the risk of partial changes.

Warnings

- Avoid locking files unnecessarily, as it may hinder team productivity.

Chapter – 13 Debugging & System Analysis

Chapter Overview

This chapter covers essential Linux commands for debugging and analyzing system performance. These commands provide insights into system calls, open files, kernel messages, memory usage, CPU performance, and system activity. Proficiency with these tools helps users diagnose and resolve system issues, analyze performance bottlenecks, and monitor system health.

Chapter Goal

- Learn to trace system calls, monitor open files, and review kernel messages.
- Understand how to analyze memory, CPU, and I/O performance.
- Gain skills to collect and report system activity information, enhancing debugging and troubleshooting capabilities.

Syntax Table

Serial No	Command	Syntax	Simple Example
1	Trace System Calls	`strace [options] [command]`	`strace ls`
2	List Open Files	`lsof [options] [file/process]`	`lsof -p 1234`

3	Print Kernel Messages	`dmesg [options]`	`` `dmesg ``
4	Report Virtual Memory Stats	`vmstat [options] [interval] [count]`	`vmstat 5 10`
5	Report CPU and I/O Stats	`iostat [options] [interval] [count]`	`iostat 5 10`
6	Report System Activity	`sar [options] [interval] [count]`	`sar -u 5 10`

Topic Explanations

1. strace - Trace System Calls and Signals

What is strace

The strace command is a diagnostic tool that traces system calls and signals for a given command or process. It helps developers and administrators debug issues by showing interactions between a program and the operating system.

Use Purpose

- **System Call Analysis**: Identifies which system calls a process makes.
- **Debugging**: Diagnoses errors and unexpected behavior in programs.

Syntax

```
strace [options] [command]
```

Syntax Explanation

- **strace**: Command to trace system calls.
    - ○ **[options]**: Configures output, such as -p to trace an existing process.
    - ○ **[command]**: The command or program to trace (e.g., ls).

Simple Code Example

```
strace ls
```

Code Example Explanation

1. **Traces** all system calls made by the `ls` command, showing each call and its result.

Common Errors and Solutions
- **Error**: `strace: command not found`
  - ○ **Solution**: Install `strace` using your package manager.

Notes
- Use `strace -o output.txt [command]` to save output to a file.

Warnings
- Extensive tracing can impact performance; avoid using `strace` on critical production services.

---

2. `lsof` - List Open Files Associated with Processes

What is `lsof`

The `lsof` command lists open files and the processes associated with them. It helps track which files are being used by a process or locate processes accessing a specific file.

Use Purpose
- **Open File Tracking**: Shows files opened by processes.
- **Resource Management**: Identifies resource usage by processes.

Syntax

```
lsof [options] [file/process]
```

Syntax Explanation
- **lsof**: Command to list open files.
  - ○ **[options]**: Common options include:
    - ■ **-p**: Lists files opened by a specific process ID.
    - ■ **+D**: Lists files in a specified directory.
  - ○ **[file/process]**: The file or process ID to filter results.

Simple Code Example

```
lsof -p 1234
```

Code Example Explanation

1. **Lists** all files opened by the process with PID 1234.

Common Errors and Solutions

*   **Error**: `lsof: command not found`
    *   **Solution**: Install `lsof` using your package manager.

Notes

*   `lsof +D /path/to/directory` lists open files in a specific directory.

Warnings

*   Avoid excessive use of `lsof` on busy servers, as it may slow down performance.

3. dmesg - Print Kernel Messages

What is dmesg

The `dmesg` command prints messages from the kernel ring buffer, which includes hardware and driver information. It's commonly used for troubleshooting hardware issues and viewing system initialization messages.

Use Purpose

*   **Kernel Message Review**: Displays messages related to hardware and system events.
*   **Debugging Hardware Issues**: Useful for identifying issues with drivers and hardware.

Syntax

```
dmesg [options]
```

Syntax Explanation

*   **dmesg**: Command to print kernel messages.
    *   **[options]**: Common options include -T to show timestamps.

Simple Code Example

```
dmesg | tail
```

Code Example Explanation

1. **Displays** the last few kernel messages, often containing recent hardware or driver logs.

Common Errors and Solutions

*   **Error**: Permission denied.
    *   **Solution**: Use `sudo dmesg` to view all messages.

Notes

- Use dmesg -w to monitor new kernel messages in real time.

Warnings

- Excessive use of dmesg may impact performance on high-activity systems.

---

4. vmstat - Report Virtual Memory Statistics

What is vmstat

The vmstat command provides reports on virtual memory, processes, I/O, and CPU usage. It helps monitor system performance and identify memory bottlenecks.

Use Purpose

- **Memory and CPU Monitoring**: Provides an overview of memory, swap, and CPU usage.
- **Performance Analysis**: Helps diagnose resource bottlenecks.

Syntax

```
vmstat [options] [interval] [count]
```

Syntax Explanation

- **vmstat**: Command for virtual memory statistics.
  - ○ **[options]**: Customizes the report, such as -s for summary output.
  - ○ **[interval]**: The time interval (in seconds) between updates.
  - ○ **[count]**: Number of updates to display.

Simple Code Example

```
vmstat 5 10
```

Code Example Explanation

1. **Displays** virtual memory stats every 5 seconds, 10 times in total.

Common Errors and Solutions

- **Error**: vmstat: command not found
  - ○ **Solution**: Install procps package (contains vmstat).

Notes

- Key fields include `si` (swap-in), `so` (swap-out), `us` (user CPU), and `sy` (system CPU).

Warnings

- Excessive use can consume resources; avoid prolonged usage on production systems.

---

5. `iostat` - Report CPU and I/O Statistics

What is `iostat`

The `iostat` command reports CPU and I/O statistics, helping users understand disk performance and identify I/O bottlenecks.

Use Purpose

- **CPU and I/O Monitoring**: Tracks CPU usage and disk I/O performance.
- **Disk Analysis**: Assesses the load on storage devices.

Syntax

```
iostat [options] [interval] [count]
```

Syntax Explanation

- **iostat**: Command for CPU and I/O statistics.
    - ○ **[options]**: Configures output (e.g., -d for device report).
    - ○ **[interval]**: The time interval (in seconds) between reports.
    - ○ **[count]**: Number of reports to generate.

Simple Code Example

```
iostat 5 10
```

Code Example Explanation

1. **Displays** CPU and I/O statistics every 5 seconds, for a total of 10 updates.

Common Errors and Solutions

- **Error**: `iostat: command not found`
    - ○ **Solution**: Install `sysstat` package (contains `iostat`).

Notes

- Important metrics include `%util` (disk utilization) and `await` (average wait time).

Warnings

- Prolonged use of `iostat` can affect performance on systems with high I/O activity.

---

6. `sar` - Collect and Report System Activity Information

What is `sar`

The `sar` command collects and reports system activity information, including CPU, memory, and network statistics. It is part of the `sysstat` package and provides historical data on system performance.

Use Purpose

- **Historical Performance Analysis**: Tracks and reports on CPU, memory, and other resources over time.
- **Detailed Monitoring**: Collects data at specified intervals for long-term analysis.

Syntax

```
sar [options] [interval] [count]
```

Syntax Explanation

- **sar**: Command to report system activity.
  - ○ **[options]**: Defines the type of report (e.g., -u for CPU usage).
  - ○ **[interval]**: The time interval (in seconds) between reports.
  - ○ **[count]**: Number of reports to generate.

Simple Code Example

```
sar -u 5 10
```

Code Example Explanation

1. **Displays** CPU usage statistics every 5 seconds, for a total of 10 reports.

Common Errors and Solutions

- **Error**: `Cannot open /var/log/sa/saXX: No such file or directory`
  - ○ **Solution**: Ensure `sysstat` is installed and configured.

Chapter – 14 Security & Permissions

Chapter Overview

This chapter introduces essential Linux commands for managing security, access control, and user monitoring. These commands help administrators secure the system by managing permissions, configuring firewalls, controlling user access, and auditing user activity. Understanding these commands is crucial for protecting a Linux environment from unauthorized access and managing secure operations.

Chapter Goal

- Learn to control access using sudo, configure firewalls with iptables and ufw, and manage SELinux contexts.
- Understand how to monitor user activity and access history with commands like last, who, and w.
- Gain skills to implement and monitor security measures, ensuring system integrity.

Syntax Table

Serial No	Command	Syntax	Simple Example
1	Execute with Privileges	sudo [command]	sudo apt update
2	Configure Packet Filtering	iptables [options]	iptables - L
3	Simplified Firewall	ufw [command]	ufw enable
4	Manage SELinux Contexts	selinux [options]	sestatus
5	Show Last Logged-In Users	last [options]	last

6	Display Logged-In Users	who [options]	who
7	Show Users and Activity	w [options]	w

Topic Explanations

1. sudo - Execute Commands with Elevated Privileges

What is sudo

The sudo command allows users to execute commands with elevated privileges, typically as the root user. It helps enforce security by controlling which users can perform administrative tasks.

Use Purpose

- **Privilege Escalation**: Allows regular users to run commands with root privileges.
- **Access Control**: Grants limited administrative access based on configuration.

Syntax

```
sudo [command]
```

Syntax Explanation

- **sudo**: Command to run with elevated privileges.
    - **[command]**: The command to execute with root access (e.g., apt update).

Simple Code Example

```
sudo apt update
```

Code Example Explanation

1. **Executes** the apt update command with root privileges, updating package lists.

Common Errors and Solutions

- **Error**: user is not in the sudoers file
    - **Solution**: Add the user to the sudoers file or group.

Notes

- Use sudo -i to open a root shell.

Warnings

- Avoid running unnecessary commands with sudo to minimize security risks.

2. iptables - Configure IP Packet Filtering Rules

What is iptables

The `iptables` command configures rules for filtering network packets on Linux, acting as a firewall. It enables administrators to control incoming and outgoing traffic based on IP, protocol, port, and more.

Use Purpose

- **Firewall Configuration**: Manages traffic by setting up packet filtering rules.
- **Network Security**: Controls access to services based on IP and port filtering.

Syntax

```
iptables [options]
```

Syntax Explanation

- **iptables**: Command to manage firewall rules.
    - ○ **[options]**: Configures the action, such as:
        - ■ **-L**: Lists current rules.
        - ■ **-A**: Adds a new rule.
        - ■ **-D**: Deletes a rule.

Simple Code Example

```
iptables -L
```

Code Example Explanation

1. **Lists** all current iptables rules, showing how network traffic is managed.

Common Errors and Solutions

- **Error**: `iptables: command not found`
    - ○ **Solution**: Install `iptables` or use `nftables` as a replacement.

Notes

- `iptables -A INPUT -p tcp --dport 80 -j ACCEPT` allows HTTP traffic on port 80.

Warnings

- Misconfigured rules can block access to critical services; test changes carefully.

3. ufw - Simplified Firewall Tool for Ubuntu/Debian

What is ufw

The ufw (Uncomplicated Firewall) command is a simplified front-end for iptables on Debian-based systems. It provides an easy interface for managing firewall rules.

Use Purpose

- **Firewall Management**: Simplifies firewall configuration for users.
- **Access Control**: Controls incoming and outgoing traffic with simple commands.

Syntax

```
ufw [command]
```

Syntax Explanation

- **ufw**: Command to manage the firewall.
  - ○ **[command]**: Actions like enable, disable, allow [port], or deny [port].

Simple Code Example

```
ufw enable
```

Code Example Explanation

1. **Enables** the firewall, applying any configured rules to control traffic.

Common Errors and Solutions

- **Error**: ufw: command not found
  - ○ **Solution**: Install ufw with sudo apt install ufw.

Notes

- Use ufw status to check the firewall status and current rules.

Warnings

- Avoid using both ufw and direct iptables commands simultaneously to prevent conflicts.

4. selinux - Manage SELinux Contexts

What is selinux

SELinux (Security-Enhanced Linux) provides a mechanism for enforcing access control policies based on security contexts. The selinux command and related tools manage SELinux status and contexts.

Use Purpose

- **Access Control**: Enforces stricter access control policies based on SELinux contexts.
- **Enhanced Security**: Provides granular control over file, process, and network access.

Syntax

```
selinux [options]
```

Syntax Explanation

- **selinux**: Command to manage SELinux settings (often accessed via sestatus).
    - ○ **[options]**: Configures SELinux, such as sestatus to check status.

Simple Code Example

```
sestatus
```

Code Example Explanation

1. **Displays** the current status of SELinux, showing whether it's enforcing, permissive, or disabled.

Common Errors and Solutions

- **Error**: SELinux is disabled
    - ○ **Solution**: Enable SELinux in the system configuration if required.

Notes

- Use chcon and semanage commands for detailed context management.

Warnings

- Misconfiguring SELinux policies can lock users out of services; test changes carefully.

5. last - Show Last Logged-In Users
What is last
The last command displays information about the most recent user logins, reboots, and shutdowns, providing a log of user activity.
Use Purpose
- **User Audit**: Shows historical login information for monitoring user access.
- **Security Tracking**: Helps identify unauthorized access by reviewing login history.
Syntax
```
last [options]
```
Syntax Explanation
- **last**: Command to display recent login information.
    - **[options]**: Customizes output (e.g., -n to limit entries).
Simple Code Example
```
last
```
Code Example Explanation
1. **Lists** the most recent logins, including user names, login times, and durations.
Common Errors and Solutions
- **Error**: Missing records in older logs.
    - **Solution**: Verify that logging is configured properly for user sessions.
Notes
- Use last -n 5 to show the last 5 login records only.
Warnings
- Regularly review login logs to identify suspicious access patterns.

---

6. who - Display Who is Logged In
What is who
The who command shows currently logged-in users, including their usernames, login times, and terminal locations.

Use Purpose
- **Session Monitoring**: Provides a list of active user sessions.
- **Access Control**: Identifies which users are currently accessing the system.

Syntax
```
who [options]
```

Syntax Explanation
- **who**: Command to list active user sessions.
    - ○ **[options]**: Customizes output (e.g., -q for quick user count).

Simple Code Example
```
who
```

Code Example Explanation
1. **Displays** all users currently logged into the system, along with login times.

Common Errors and Solutions
- **Error**: None commonly encountered with who.

Notes
- Use who -q to show only the user count and names.

Warnings
- Monitor user sessions to ensure only authorized users have access.

7. w - Show Who is Logged On and What They Are Doing

What is w
The w command shows details about logged-in users and their activities, including uptime, load averages, and CPU usage.

Use Purpose
- **User Activity Monitoring**: Shows active users and their current actions.
- **System Load Monitoring**: Provides load averages and resource usage.

Syntax
```
w [options]
```

Syntax Explanation

- **w**: Command to display active users and load information.
  - ○ **[options]**: Configures output (rarely used).

Simple Code Example

```
w
```

Code Example Explanation

1. **Displays** logged-in users, their active processes, and system load information.

Common Errors and Solutions

- **Error**: None commonly encountered with w.

Notes

- The command output includes details like idle time and active commands.

Warnings

- High load averages may indicate that the system is under stress; monitor resource usage closely.

Chapter – 15 Backup & Restore

Chapter Overview

This chapter covers essential Linux commands for backing up and restoring files, directories, and entire disks. These commands provide methods for synchronizing data, creating compressed archives, cloning disks, and restoring backups. Mastering these tools helps users protect data and recover it in case of system failures or data loss.

Chapter Goal

- Learn to synchronize files and directories with rsync, clone disks with dd, and create compressed archives with tar.
- Understand how to restore files from backups using restore and manage data protection.
- Gain skills to efficiently back up critical data and ensure reliable restoration.

Syntax Table

Seria l No	Command	Syntax	Simple Example
1	Synchronize Files	rsync [options] [source] [destination]	rsync -av /src /dest
2	Disk Cloning Utility	dd [options]	dd if=/dev/sda of=/dev/sdb
3	Archive and Compress	tar [options] [archive_name] [files]	tar -cvf backup.tar /path/to/files
4	Restore from Backup	restore [options] [files]	restore -rf /backup/dumpfil e

Topic Explanations

1. rsync - Synchronize Files and Directories Efficiently

What is rsync

The rsync command synchronizes files and directories between two locations, either locally or remotely. It is highly efficient, transferring only changed data and reducing bandwidth usage.

Use Purpose

- **Efficient File Synchronization**: Synchronizes files and directories while transferring only changes.
- **Backup Automation**: Enables incremental backups for efficient storage.

Syntax

```
rsync [options] [source] [destination]
```

Syntax Explanation

- **rsync**: Command for file synchronization.
  - ○ **[options]**: Configures behavior, such as:
    - ■ **-a**: Enables archive mode, preserving permissions.
    - ■ **-v**: Verbose output.
  - ○ **[source]**: The source file or directory to synchronize.
  - ○ **[destination]**: The target location for synchronization.

Simple Code Example

```
rsync -av /src /dest
```

Code Example Explanation

1. **Synchronizes** the /src directory with /dest, preserving file attributes and showing verbose output.

Common Errors and Solutions

- **Error**: rsync: command not found
  - ○ **Solution**: Install rsync using your package manager (e.g., sudo apt install rsync).

Notes

- Use rsync -a --delete /src /dest to remove files in the destination that are no longer in the source.

2. dd - Low-Level Copying and Conversion Utility

What is dd

The dd command copies and converts data at a low level, often used for disk cloning, creating bootable USB drives, or making disk backups. It operates at the byte level and is extremely powerful.

Use Purpose

- **Disk Cloning**: Creates a full copy of a disk or partition.
- **Data Conversion**: Converts file formats, such as encoding and block sizes.

Syntax

```
dd [options]
```

Syntax Explanation

- **dd**: Command for low-level copying and conversion.
  - ○ **[options]**: Configures input, output, and data handling, such as:
    - ■ **if=**: Specifies the input file (source).
    - ■ **of=**: Specifies the output file (destination).
    - ■ **bs=**: Sets the block size (e.g., bs=4M for 4 MB blocks).

Simple Code Example

```
dd if=/dev/sda of=/dev/sdb bs=4M
```

Code Example Explanation

1. **Clones** the contents of the /dev/sda disk to /dev/sdb, copying data in 4 MB blocks.

Common Errors and Solutions

- **Error**: Permission denied.
  - ○ **Solution**: Run dd with sudo for necessary permissions.

Notes

- Use caution when specifying if and of, as reversing them can lead to data loss.

Warnings

- dd is a powerful tool that can overwrite data without warning; double-check command syntax.

3. `tar` - Archive and Compress Files for Backup

What is `tar`

The `tar` command creates compressed or uncompressed archive files, combining multiple files or directories into a single file for easy backup, storage, or transfer.

Use Purpose

- **File Archiving**: Bundles multiple files into a single archive.
- **Compression**: Reduces file size for efficient storage and transfer.

Syntax

```
tar [options] [archive_name] [files]
```

Syntax Explanation

- **tar**: Command to create or extract archives.
  - **[options]**: Configures operation, such as:
    - **-c**: Creates a new archive.
    - **-v**: Verbose output, listing files.
    - **-f**: Specifies the archive file name.
    - **-z**: Compresses with gzip.
  - **[archive_name]**: Name of the output archive file (e.g., `backup.tar.gz`).
  - **[files]**: Files or directories to include in the archive.

Simple Code Example

```
tar -cvf backup.tar /path/to/files
```

Code Example Explanation

1. **Creates** an archive named `backup.tar` containing all files in `/path/to/files`.

Common Errors and Solutions

- **Error**: `tar: permission denied`
  - **Solution**: Use `sudo` if necessary for restricted files.

Notes

- Use `tar -xvf backup.tar` to extract an archive.

Warnings

- Including `-P` option with tar preserves absolute paths, which may not be desired when restoring.

4. restore - Restore Files from a Backup

What is restore

The `restore` command restores files from backups created with dump, a command used for full and incremental backups on Linux systems. It allows selective restoration or full recovery.

Use Purpose

- **File Restoration**: Restores specific files or entire directories from a backup.
- **System Recovery**: Reverts to previous states in case of data loss or corruption.

Syntax

```
restore [options] [files]
```

Syntax Explanation

- **restore**: Command to restore files from a backup.
  - ○ **[options]**: Configures restoration, such as:
    - ■ **-r**: Restores the entire backup.
    - ■ **-i**: Interactive mode for selective restoration.
  - ○ **[files]**: The backup file or files to restore (e.g., `/backup/dumpfile`).

Simple Code Example

```
restore -rf /backup/dumpfile
```

Code Example Explanation

1. **Restores** the entire backup from `/backup/dumpfile`, overwriting current files.

Common Errors and Solutions

- **Error**: `restore: command not found`
  - ○ **Solution**: Ensure that dump and `restore` are installed.

Notes

- Interactive mode (-i) allows restoring selected files rather than the entire backup.

Warnings

- Be cautious when restoring as it can overwrite current files without prompting.

Chapter – 16 Virtualization & Containers

Chapter Overview

This chapter covers essential Linux tools for managing virtual machines and containerized applications. These tools enable users to create, deploy, and manage containers and virtual machines, providing flexible and scalable environments for development and production. Understanding these tools is key for efficient management and orchestration in cloud and containerized infrastructure.

Chapter Goal

- Learn to manage Docker containers, images, and multi-container applications with docker and docker-compose.
- Understand Kubernetes cluster management with kubectl.
- Gain skills to handle virtual machines using virt-manager and virsh.

Syntax Table

Serial No	Command	Syntax	Simple Example
1	Manage Docker Containers	docker [command] [options]	docker run -d nginx
2	Multi-Container Applications	docker-compose [command]	docker-compose up
3	Kubernetes Management	kubectl [command] [resource] [options]	kubectl get pods
4	Manage Virtual Machines (GUI)	virt-manager	virt-manager

| 5 | Manage Virtual Machines (CLI) | `virsh [command] [options]` | `virsh start vm_name` |

Topic Explanations

1. docker - Manage Docker Containers and Images

What is docker

The docker command allows users to manage containerized applications by creating, running, stopping, and managing Docker containers and images. Docker provides a lightweight, portable environment for application development and deployment.

Use Purpose

- **Container Management**: Runs, stops, and monitors containers.
- **Image Management**: Builds, pulls, and pushes container images.

Syntax

```
docker [command] [options]
```

Syntax Explanation

- **docker**: Command to interact with Docker.
  - **[command]**: Specifies the Docker action, such as run, stop, or pull.
  - **[options]**: Configures command behavior, e.g., -d for detached mode.

Simple Code Example

```
docker run -d nginx
```

Code Example Explanation

1. **Runs** an nginx container in detached mode, allowing it to run in the background.

Common Errors and Solutions

- **Error**: Cannot connect to the Docker daemon
  - **Solution**: Ensure Docker is installed and the service is running.

Notes

- Use docker ps to list running containers and docker images to view available images.

Warnings

- Avoid running containers with --privileged unless necessary, as it may expose security risks.

2. docker-compose - Define and Run Multi-Container Docker Applications

What is docker-compose

The docker-compose command is a tool for defining and managing multi-container Docker applications using a docker-compose.yml file. It simplifies starting, stopping, and orchestrating containers.

Use Purpose

- **Multi-Container Setup**: Defines services, networks, and volumes in a single file.
- **Simplified Orchestration**: Manages multiple containers with a single command.

Syntax

```
docker-compose [command]
```

Syntax Explanation

- **docker-compose**: Command to manage multi-container applications.
  - ○ **[command]**: Actions like up, down, or build.

Simple Code Example

```
docker-compose up
```

Code Example Explanation

1. **Starts** all containers defined in the docker-compose.yml file.

Common Errors and Solutions

- **Error**: docker-compose: command not found
  - ○ **Solution**: Install Docker Compose using the Docker website or package manager.

Notes
- Use docker-compose down to stop and remove all containers, networks, and volumes defined in the configuration.

Warnings
- Misconfigured docker-compose.yml files can lead to unexpected application behavior.

---

3. kubectl - Kubernetes Command-Line Interface for Managing Clusters

What is kubectl

The kubectl command is the command-line interface for interacting with Kubernetes clusters. It manages resources like pods, deployments, and services within the cluster.

Use Purpose
- **Cluster Management**: Manages Kubernetes resources such as pods, services, and deployments.
- **Deployment Scaling**: Adjusts the scale of applications within a cluster.

Syntax

```
kubectl [command] [resource] [options]
```

Syntax Explanation
- **kubectl**: Command to manage Kubernetes clusters.
    - **[command]**: Specifies the action, such as get, apply, or delete.
    - **[resource]**: Defines the Kubernetes resource, like pod, service, or deployment.
    - **[options]**: Additional options to refine the command.

Simple Code Example

```
kubectl get pods
```

Code Example Explanation
1. **Lists** all pods in the current Kubernetes namespace, providing an overview of application instances.

Common Errors and Solutions
- **Error**: The connection to the server was refused

   ○ **Solution**: Ensure the Kubernetes cluster is running and configured correctly.

Notes

- Use `kubectl apply -f config.yaml` to apply changes from a configuration file.

Warnings

- Changes made with `kubectl` are immediate; test configurations in a staging environment first.

---

4. `virt-manager` - GUI Tool for Managing Virtual Machines

What is `virt-manager`

The `virt-manager` (Virtual Machine Manager) is a graphical tool for managing virtual machines. It simplifies creating, configuring, and monitoring VMs with a user-friendly interface.

Use Purpose

- **Graphical VM Management**: Provides an easy-to-use GUI for managing VMs.
- **VM Monitoring**: Allows real-time monitoring of VM performance.

Syntax

```
virt-manager
```

Syntax Explanation

- **virt-manager**: Opens the Virtual Machine Manager application, which displays a graphical interface for managing VMs.

Simple Code Example

```
virt-manager
```

Code Example Explanation

1. **Launches** the `virt-manager` GUI, allowing users to create, start, and monitor virtual machines.

Common Errors and Solutions

- **Error**: `virt-manager: command not found`

- Solution: Install `virt-manager` using your package manager (e.g., `sudo apt install virt-manager`).

Notes
- `virt-manager` works with `libvirt`, so ensure the `libvirtd` daemon is running.

Warnings
- Network misconfigurations in `virt-manager` may isolate VMs from the host or other networks.

5. `virsh` - Command-Line Interface for Managing Virtual Machines

What is `virsh`

The `virsh` command-line tool manages virtual machines on systems that use the `libvirt` virtualization API. It provides powerful command-line options for VM creation, management, and monitoring.

Use Purpose
- **CLI VM Management**: Allows users to start, stop, and configure VMs from the command line.
- **Automation**: Supports scripting for automating VM tasks.

Syntax

```
virsh [command] [options]
```

Syntax Explanation
- **virsh**: Command-line tool to manage VMs.
  - **[command]**: Specifies the VM action, such as `start`, `shutdown`, or `list`.
  - **[options]**: Additional parameters to customize the command.

Simple Code Example

```
virsh start vm_name
```

Code Example Explanation
1. **Starts** the specified virtual machine, identified by vm_name.

Common Errors and Solutions

- **Error**: `error: Failed to connect to the hypervisor`
  - **Solution**: Ensure `libvirtd` is running and you have the necessary permissions.

Notes

- Use `virsh list --all` to see all VMs, including stopped ones.

Warnings

- Avoid force-stopping critical VMs, as this can lead to data loss or corruption.

Chapter – 17 Shell Scripting & Automation

Chapter Overview

This chapter covers essential commands for shell scripting and automation in Linux. Shell scripting enables users to automate repetitive tasks, create powerful command-line tools, and manage system operations efficiently. The commands here include foundational shell utilities like bash and zsh, along with scripting essentials such as alias, source, and test.

Chapter Goal

- Learn the basics of shell scripting using bash and zsh.
- Understand how to create command shortcuts with alias and execute scripts with source.
- Gain skills to automate tasks and add conditional logic with test.

Syntax Table

Serial No	Command	Syntax	Simple Example
1	Standard Linux Shell	bash [options] [script]	bash myscript.sh
2	Advanced Shell	zsh [options] [script]	zsh myscript.sh
3	Command Shortcuts	alias [name]='[command]'	alias ll='ls -la'
4	Run Script in Current Shell	source [filename]	source ~/.bashrc
5	Conditional Expressions	test [expression]	test -f myfile.txt

Topic Explanations

1. bash - Bourne Again SHell, Standard Linux Shell

What is bash

The bash command starts the Bourne Again SHell, the default shell on most Linux systems. It is widely used for scripting and command-line interaction, offering features like variables, functions, and control structures.

Use Purpose

- **Interactive Shell**: Provides a command-line interface for user interaction.
- **Script Execution**: Runs shell scripts for task automation.

Syntax

```
bash [options] [script]
```

Syntax Explanation

- **bash**: Command to start the Bourne Again SHell.
  - ○ **[options]**: Configures behavior, such as -c to run a command.
  - ○ **[script]**: Specifies the shell script to execute.

Simple Code Example

```
bash myscript.sh
```

Code Example Explanation

1. **Executes** myscript.sh in a new instance of the bash shell.

Common Errors and Solutions

- **Error**: bash: myscript.sh: command not found
  - ○ **Solution**: Ensure the script is in the current directory or provide the full path.

Notes

- Use #!/bin/bash at the top of a script to specify bash as the interpreter.

Warnings

- Ensure scripts have executable permissions with chmod +x scriptname.sh.

2. zsh - Z Shell, an Advanced Shell with Many Features

What is zsh

The zsh command starts the Z shell, an advanced shell offering enhanced features over bash, including improved autocompletion, theme support, and scripting capabilities.

Use Purpose

- **Enhanced Command-Line Experience**: Provides a more interactive shell experience.
- **Advanced Scripting**: Allows use of advanced features and plugins.

Syntax

```
zsh [options] [script]
```

Syntax Explanation

- **zsh**: Command to start the Z shell.
  - **[options]**: Configures behavior, such as -c to run a command.
  - **[script]**: The script to execute using zsh.

Simple Code Example

```
zsh myscript.sh
```

Code Example Explanation

1. **Executes** myscript.sh in the Z shell, taking advantage of zsh-specific features.

Common Errors and Solutions

- **Error**: zsh: command not found
  - **Solution**: Install zsh using your package manager (e.g., sudo apt install zsh).

Notes

- zsh is highly customizable and works well with tools like oh-my-zsh.

Warnings

- Some bash-specific scripts may not be compatible with zsh.

3. `alias` - Set Shortcuts for Commands

What is `alias`

The `alias` command allows users to create shortcuts for longer or frequently used commands. Aliases make the command line more efficient by reducing the need to type repetitive commands.

Use Purpose

- **Command Shortcuts**: Creates simple shortcuts for commonly used commands.
- **Customization**: Personalizes the shell environment to improve workflow.

Syntax

```
alias [name]='[command]'
```

Syntax Explanation

- **alias**: Command to set a shortcut.
    - ○ **[name]**: The name of the alias.
    - ○ **[command]**: The full command to run when the alias is used.

Simple Code Example

```
alias ll='ls -la'
```

Code Example Explanation

1. **Creates** an alias `ll` that runs `ls -la`, listing files with detailed information.

Common Errors and Solutions

- **Error**: `alias: not found`
    - ○ **Solution**: Ensure the command syntax is correct; aliases cannot contain spaces around the equals sign.

Notes

- Add aliases to `~/.bashrc` or `~/.zshrc` for persistence across sessions.

Warnings

- Avoid using aliases that override essential system commands.

4. source - Run a Script in the Current Shell

What is source

The source command executes a script in the current shell rather than starting a new shell. This is especially useful for scripts that set environment variables or change the current directory.

Use Purpose

- **Environment Sourcing**: Loads variables and functions into the current shell session.
- **Configuration Reloading**: Reloads configuration files like .bashrc or .zshrc.

Syntax

```
source [filename]
```

Syntax Explanation

- **source**: Command to run a script in the current shell.
  - **[filename]**: The script file to execute.

Simple Code Example

```
source ~/.bashrc
```

Code Example Explanation

1. **Reloads** the .bashrc file, applying any recent changes to environment variables or aliases.

Common Errors and Solutions

- **Error**: No such file or directory
  - **Solution**: Verify the file path and file name.

Notes

- source can be shortened to . in most shells (e.g., . ~/.bashrc).

Warnings

- Be cautious with sourced scripts, as they can modify the current shell environment.

5. `test` - Evaluate Conditional Expressions

What is `test`

The `test` command evaluates conditional expressions, allowing scripts to perform logical checks and make decisions based on file existence, string comparison, or numerical conditions.

Use Purpose

- **Conditional Logic**: Enables decision-making within shell scripts.
- **File and String Checks**: Verifies file existence, permissions, and string matches.

Syntax

```
test [expression]
```

Syntax Explanation

- **test**: Command to evaluate a conditional expression.
  - **[expression]**: The condition to test, such as `-f [file]` to check if a file exists.

Simple Code Example

```
test -f myfile.txt
```

Code Example Explanation

1. **Checks** if `myfile.txt` exists as a file; returns 0 (success) if true.

Common Errors and Solutions

- **Error**: Incorrect test expression syntax.
  - **Solution**: Verify that brackets and operators are used correctly.

Notes

- Often written as `[ expression ]`, which is more common in scripts (e.g., `[ -f myfile.txt ]`).

Warnings

- Double-check expressions, as incorrect conditions can lead to unexpected script behavior.

Chapter – 18 System Performance Monitoring

Chapter Overview

This chapter introduces essential Linux commands for monitoring system performance, including CPU, network, and disk usage. These tools provide real-time data to diagnose system issues, optimize resource usage, and troubleshoot performance bottlenecks. Proficiency with these commands helps ensure that applications run smoothly and resources are managed efficiently.

Chapter Goal

- Learn to monitor application performance with `perf`, network usage with `nload` and `iftop`, and disk I/O with `iotop`.
- Understand how to analyze CPU usage per processor with `mpstat`.
- Gain skills to track and diagnose performance issues, making informed adjustments to optimize system performance.

Syntax Table

Serial No	Command	Syntax	Simple Example
1	Application Profiling	`perf [command] [options]`	`perf stat ls`
2	Network Bandwidth Usage	`nload [options]`	`nload`
3	Disk I/O Usage	`iotop [options]`	`iotop`
4	Real-Time Network Monitoring	`iftop [options]`	`iftop`
5	CPU Usage per Processor	`mpstat [options] [interval] [count]`	`mpstat 5 10`

Topic Explanations

1. perf - Performance Monitoring for Profiling Applications

What is perf

The perf command is a performance monitoring tool that profiles applications, tracking events like CPU cycles, cache references, and memory loads. It helps developers and administrators analyze application performance and identify bottlenecks.

Use Purpose

- **Application Profiling**: Monitors performance metrics such as CPU cycles and memory usage.
- **Optimization**: Identifies inefficient code sections and potential bottlenecks.

Syntax

```
perf [command] [options]
```

Syntax Explanation

- **perf**: Command for profiling application performance.
    - ○ **[command]**: Specifies the perf command, such as stat or record.
    - ○ **[options]**: Additional configuration options (e.g., -a for system-wide monitoring).

Simple Code Example

```
perf stat ls
```

Code Example Explanation

1. **Profiles** the ls command, providing statistics such as CPU cycles and instructions.

Common Errors and Solutions

- **Error**: perf: command not found
    - ○ **Solution**: Install perf with your package manager (e.g., sudo apt install linux-tools-common).

Notes

- Use perf record to capture data and perf report to analyze it afterward.

2. nload - Monitor Network Bandwidth Usage in Real-Time

What is nload

The `nload` command provides a visual display of real-time network bandwidth usage. It shows incoming and outgoing traffic, helping administrators monitor network activity and detect bandwidth issues.

Use Purpose

- **Network Monitoring**: Tracks real-time bandwidth usage on network interfaces.
- **Traffic Analysis**: Helps identify unusual network traffic patterns.

Syntax

```
nload [options]
```

Syntax Explanation

- **nload**: Command to monitor network traffic.
    - **[options]**: Configures display settings, such as -m to monitor multiple interfaces.

Simple Code Example

```
nload
```

Code Example Explanation

1. **Launches** a visual display showing real-time network bandwidth usage on the default network interface.

Common Errors and Solutions

- **Error**: nload: command not found
    - **Solution**: Install nload using your package manager (e.g., sudo apt install nload).

Notes

- Use arrow keys to switch between network interfaces.

Warnings

- nload is best suited for interactive use, as it doesn't log data.

3. `iotop` - Display Disk I/O Usage by Processes

What is `iotop`

The `iotop` command shows real-time disk I/O usage by individual processes, helping administrators identify processes consuming excessive disk resources.

Use Purpose

- **Disk Usage Monitoring**: Provides insights into disk I/O for each running process.
- **Resource Management**: Helps identify I/O bottlenecks caused by specific applications.

Syntax

```
iotop [options]
```

Syntax Explanation

- **iotop**: Command to display disk I/O by process.
    - **[options]**: Configures output, such as -o to show only active processes.

Simple Code Example

```
iotop
```

Code Example Explanation

1. **Displays** real-time disk I/O usage for processes, showing read and write speeds.

Common Errors and Solutions

- **Error**: `iotop: command not found`
    - **Solution**: Install `iotop` with your package manager (e.g., `sudo apt install iotop`).

Notes

- Use `iotop -o` to display only processes actively performing I/O.

Warnings

- Requires root privileges; use `sudo` to run.

4. `iftop` - Real-Time Network Bandwidth Monitoring

What is `iftop`

The `iftop` command provides real-time monitoring of network bandwidth usage, displaying active connections and traffic flow by IP address.

Use Purpose

- **Connection Monitoring**: Shows real-time bandwidth usage by individual connections.
- **Traffic Analysis**: Helps detect suspicious or high-traffic connections.

Syntax

```
iftop [options]
```

Syntax Explanation

- **iftop**: Command for real-time network monitoring.
    - **[options]**: Customizes output, such as -i to specify an interface.

Simple Code Example

```
iftop
```

Code Example Explanation

1. **Displays** real-time bandwidth usage for each active connection on the default network interface.

Common Errors and Solutions

- **Error**: `iftop: command not found`
    - **Solution**: Install `iftop` using the package manager (e.g., `sudo apt install iftop`).

Notes

- Use `iftop -i eth0` to monitor a specific interface, such as `eth0`.

Warnings

- Requires root privileges; use `sudo` to run.

5. mpstat - CPU Usage Per Processor

What is mpstat

The mpstat command reports CPU usage for each processor. It is useful for identifying CPU bottlenecks and observing the load distribution across processors.

Use Purpose

- **CPU Monitoring**: Displays CPU usage statistics per processor or core.
- **Load Balancing**: Helps assess load distribution across multiple processors.

Syntax

```
mpstat [options] [interval] [count]
```

Syntax Explanation

- **mpstat**: Command to display CPU usage statistics.
    - ○ **[options]**: Configures output, such as -P to specify individual processors.
    - ○ **[interval]**: Time in seconds between updates.
    - ○ **[count]**: Number of updates to display.

Simple Code Example

```
mpstat 5 10
```

Code Example Explanation

1. **Displays** CPU usage for each processor every 5 seconds, for a total of 10 updates.

Common Errors and Solutions

- **Error**: mpstat: command not found
    - ○ **Solution**: Install sysstat package (contains mpstat).

Notes

- Key metrics include %usr (user CPU), %sys (system CPU), and %idle (idle time).

Warnings

- mpstat data may consume resources on systems with many processors; use sparingly.

Chapter – 19 Network Management

Chapter Overview

This chapter covers essential Linux commands for managing and troubleshooting network connections. These commands provide tools for configuring network interfaces, scanning networks, analyzing packets, managing ARP caches, and viewing routing tables. Mastery of these tools is essential for ensuring network connectivity, diagnosing network issues, and securing network traffic.

Chapter Goal

- Learn to configure network interfaces and routes with `ip` and `route`.
- Understand how to explore networks and scan ports using `nmap`.
- Gain skills to analyze network traffic with `tcpdump` and manage ARP caches with `arp`.

Syntax Table

Serial No	Command	Syntax	Simple Example
1	Network Interface Configuration	`ip [object] [command] [options]`	`ip addr show`
2	Network Exploration & Security	`nmap [options] [target]`	`nmap 192.168.1.1`
3	Packet Analysis	`tcpdump [options]`	`tcpdump -i eth0`
4	ARP Cache Management	`arp [options]`	`arp -a`

5	IP Routing Table Manipulation	`route [options]`	`route -n`

Topic Explanations

1. `ip` - Advanced Tool for Configuring Network Interfaces, Routing Tables, and Tunnels

What is `ip`

The `ip` command is a powerful tool for configuring network interfaces, managing IP addresses, setting up routing tables, and configuring tunnels. It is part of the `iproute2` package, replacing older tools like `ifconfig`.

Use Purpose

- **Network Interface Configuration**: Adds, removes, and displays network interfaces.
- **Routing Management**: Configures and displays IP routing tables.

Syntax

```
ip [object] [command] [options]
```

Syntax Explanation

- **ip**: Command to manage network configurations.
  - **[object]**: Network object to manage, such as `addr` (address) or `route`.
  - **[command]**: Action to perform, such as `show`, `add`, or `del`.
  - **[options]**: Additional options, such as `dev` to specify an interface.

Simple Code Example

```
ip addr show
```

Code Example Explanation

1. **Displays** IP addresses and other details of all network interfaces.

Common Errors and Solutions

- **Error**: `ip: command not found`
  - ○ **Solution**: Install `iproute2` using the package manager (e.g., `sudo apt install iproute2`).

Notes
- Use `ip link show` to see network interface status and `ip route` to view routing information.

Warnings
- Modifying routes and interfaces without understanding may lead to loss of network connectivity.

---

2. nmap - Network Exploration Tool and Security/Port Scanner

What is nmap

The nmap command is a powerful network exploration tool and security scanner. It allows administrators to discover hosts and services, perform network inventory, and identify open ports on target systems.

Use Purpose
- **Network Scanning**: Detects active hosts, services, and open ports.
- **Security Auditing**: Identifies potential vulnerabilities and weak points in network security.

Syntax

```
nmap [options] [target]
```

Syntax Explanation
- **nmap**: Command to perform network scanning.
  - ○ **[options]**: Configures scan behavior, such as `-sS` for stealth scan.
  - ○ **[target]**: IP address or hostname to scan.

Simple Code Example

```
nmap 192.168.1.1
```

Code Example Explanation
1. **Performs** a basic scan on IP address `192.168.1.1`, listing open ports and services.

Common Errors and Solutions
- **Error**: `nmap: command not found`

○ **Solution**: Install nmap using the package manager (e.g., `sudo apt install nmap`).

Notes

- Use `nmap -A [target]` for a more detailed scan, including OS and service detection.

Warnings

- Ensure you have authorization to scan target networks; unauthorized scanning can violate policies or laws.

---

3. `tcpdump` - Command-Line Packet Analyzer

What is `tcpdump`

The `tcpdump` command captures and analyzes network packets on interfaces, allowing administrators to examine traffic flow and troubleshoot network issues.

Use Purpose

- **Packet Capture**: Captures packets in real-time for analysis.
- **Network Troubleshooting**: Diagnoses network problems by analyzing packet data.

Syntax

```
tcpdump [options]
```

Syntax Explanation

- **tcpdump**: Command for packet capture and analysis.
  ○ **[options]**: Configures capture behavior, such as `-i` to specify an interface or `-w` to save output to a file.

Simple Code Example

```
tcpdump -i eth0
```

Code Example Explanation

1. **Captures** and displays network packets on the `eth0` interface in real-time.

Common Errors and Solutions

- **Error**: `tcpdump : command not found`
  ○ **Solution**: Install `tcpdump` using the package manager (e.g., `sudo apt install tcpdump`).

- Use `tcpdump -w capture.pcap` to save captured packets to a file for later analysis.

4. arp - Display or Manipulate the System ARP Cache

What is arp

The `arp` command manages the Address Resolution Protocol (ARP) cache, mapping IP addresses to MAC addresses. It is used to view and modify cached entries, which helps diagnose network connectivity issues.

Use Purpose

- **ARP Cache Management**: Views and modifies the ARP cache to manage IP-MAC mappings.
- **Network Diagnostics**: Helps troubleshoot IP-to-MAC address resolution issues.

Syntax

```
arp [options]
```

Syntax Explanation

- **arp**: Command to manage the ARP cache.
    - ○ **[options]**: Configures output or actions, such as `-a` to display all entries.

Simple Code Example

```
arp -a
```

Code Example Explanation

1. **Displays** all entries in the ARP cache, showing IP-to-MAC mappings.

Common Errors and Solutions

- **Error**: `arp: command not found`
    - ○ **Solution**: Install `net-tools` (contains `arp`) with your package manager.

Notes

- Use `arp -d [ip_address]` to delete an ARP entry.

Warnings

- Modifying the ARP cache without understanding may disrupt network communication.

5. route - Show/Manipulate IP Routing Tables

What is route

The `route` command displays and modifies the IP routing table. It helps administrators manage network routing, control default gateways, and troubleshoot connectivity issues.

Use Purpose

- **Routing Table Management**: Configures routing to control data paths in the network.
- **Network Troubleshooting**: Diagnoses routing issues and optimizes path selection.

Syntax

```
route [options]
```

Syntax Explanation

- **route**: Command to view or modify the IP routing table.
    - **[options]**: Configures action, such as -n to display IPs in numeric format.

Simple Code Example

```
route -n
```

Code Example Explanation

1. **Displays** the routing table in numeric format, showing destinations, gateways, and network interfaces.

Common Errors and Solutions

- **Error**: `route: command not found`
    - **Solution**: Install `net-tools` (contains `route`) with your package manager.

Notes

- Use `route add default gw [gateway_ip]` to set a default gateway.

Chapter – 20 Storage & Disk Utilities

Chapter Overview

This chapter covers essential Linux commands for managing storage devices and disk utilities. These tools help users list connected devices, monitor drive health, identify bad blocks, and securely erase data. Proficiency in using these tools is essential for ensuring storage integrity, troubleshooting device issues, and securely handling data.

Chapter Goal

- Learn to list USB and SCSI devices with `lsusb` and `lsscsi`.
- Understand how to monitor hard drive health with `smartctl` and check for bad blocks with `badblocks`.
- Gain skills to securely erase data with `wipe`, ensuring safe data handling.

Syntax Table

Serial No	Command	Syntax	Simple Example
1	List USB Devices	`lsusb [options]`	`lsusb`
2	Display SCSI Devices	`lsscsi [options]`	`lsscsi`
3	Securely Erase Files or Drives	`wipe [options] [file/device]`	`wipe -r /path/to/sec ure_delete`
4	Search for Bad Blocks	`badblocks [options] [device]`	`badblocks -v /dev/sda`
5	Monitor S.M.A.R.T. Status	`smartctl [options] [device]`	`smartctl -H /dev/sda`

Topic Explanations

1. lsusb - List USB Devices Connected to the System

What is lsusb

The lsusb command lists all USB devices connected to the system, providing information about the device ID, vendor, and other details. It is useful for identifying connected USB peripherals and troubleshooting USB-related issues.

Use Purpose

- **Device Identification**: Lists USB devices and displays their details.
- **Troubleshooting**: Helps identify and resolve USB connection problems.

Syntax

```
lsusb [options]
```

Syntax Explanation

- **lsusb**: Command to list USB devices.
    - **[options]**: Configures display options, such as -v for verbose output.

Simple Code Example

```
lsusb
```

Code Example Explanation

1. **Lists** all USB devices connected to the system, displaying device IDs and vendor names.

Common Errors and Solutions

- **Error**: No USB devices detected.
    - **Solution**: Verify USB connections and ensure the USB drivers are correctly installed.

Notes

- Use lsusb -v for detailed information on each USB device.

Warnings

- Be cautious when troubleshooting as incorrect handling may affect USB device performance.

2. lsscsi - Display SCSI Devices

What is lsscsi

The lsscsi command lists all SCSI devices connected to the system, such as hard drives, optical drives, and tape drives. It provides information about device types, SCSI IDs, and device paths.

Use Purpose

- **Device Detection**: Lists SCSI devices and shows device details.
- **Hardware Inventory**: Helps identify SCSI storage devices connected to the system.

Syntax

```
lsscsi [options]
```

Syntax Explanation

- **lsscsi**: Command to list SCSI devices.
    - **[options]**: Configures display options, such as -s for device size.

Simple Code Example

```
lsscsi
```

Code Example Explanation

1. **Lists** all connected SCSI devices, including details about each device's path and type.

Common Errors and Solutions

- **Error**: lsscsi: command not found
    - **Solution**: Install lsscsi using your package manager (e.g., sudo apt install lsscsi).

Notes

- Use lsscsi -l to display detailed information about each device.

Warnings

- Ensure accurate identification of devices before performing actions like formatting or wiping.

3. `wipe` - Securely Erase Files or Drives

What is `wipe`

The `wipe` command securely deletes files or entire drives, overwriting data multiple times to prevent data recovery. It is useful for ensuring that sensitive information is irretrievably erased.

Use Purpose

- **Data Security**: Permanently removes data to prevent recovery.
- **Secure Deletion**: Ensures sensitive information is completely erased.

Syntax

```
wipe [options] [file/device]
```

Syntax Explanation

- **wipe**: Command to securely erase data.
  - **[options]**: Configures wiping options, such as -r for recursive wiping of directories.
  - **[file/device]**: Specifies the file or device to be securely erased.

Simple Code Example

```
wipe -r /path/to/secure_delete
```

Code Example Explanation

1. **Recursively wipes** the contents of the specified directory, ensuring files are permanently deleted.

Common Errors and Solutions

- **Error**: wipe: command not found
  - **Solution**: Install wipe with the package manager (e.g., sudo apt install wipe).

Notes

- Use caution with wipe, as data cannot be recovered once it is erased.

Warnings

- Double-check the target file or device before running wipe, as this action is irreversible.

4. badblocks - Search for Bad Blocks on a Device

What is badblocks

The badblocks command scans a storage device for bad blocks (corrupted or unreadable sectors) and reports their location. It helps assess the health of storage devices and identify potential data loss risks.

Use Purpose

- **Disk Health Check**: Identifies unreadable sectors or bad blocks on a disk.
- **Preemptive Maintenance**: Helps detect disk issues early to prevent data loss.

Syntax

```
badblocks [options] [device]
```

Syntax Explanation

- **badblocks**: Command to check for bad blocks on a storage device.
  - **[options]**: Configures scanning options, such as -v for verbose output.
  - **[device]**: The storage device to scan (e.g., /dev/sda).

Simple Code Example

```
badblocks -v /dev/sda
```

Code Example Explanation

1. **Scans** the /dev/sda device for bad blocks, displaying progress and any bad sectors found.

Common Errors and Solutions

- **Error**: Permission denied.
  - **Solution**: Run badblocks with sudo to allow access to disk devices.

Notes

- Consider redirecting output to a file for record-keeping (e.g., badblocks -v /dev/sda > badblocks.log).

Warnings

- badblocks may take time to complete on large disks; avoid interruptions.

5. `smartctl` - Monitor S.M.A.R.T. Health Status of Hard Drives

What is `smartctl`

The `smartctl` command is part of the `smartmontools` package and allows users to monitor the S.M.A.R.T. (Self-Monitoring, Analysis, and Reporting Technology) health status of hard drives. It provides detailed drive health information and diagnostic data.

Use Purpose

- **Drive Health Monitoring**: Checks S.M.A.R.T. data to assess drive health.
- **Failure Prediction**: Provides early warnings for potential drive failures.

Syntax

```
smartctl [options] [device]
```

Syntax Explanation

- **smartctl**: Command to interact with S.M.A.R.T. features on storage devices.
    - **[options]**: Configures output, such as -H for a health check or -a for detailed information.
    - **[device]**: Specifies the drive to check (e.g., /dev/sda).

Simple Code Example

```
smartctl -H /dev/sda
```

Code Example Explanation

1. **Performs** a quick health check on the /dev/sda drive, indicating if the drive is healthy or likely to fail.

Common Errors and Solutions

- **Error**: `smartctl: command not found`
    - **Solution**: Install `smartmontools` (e.g., `sudo apt install smartmontools`).

Notes

- Use `smartctl -a /dev/sda` for a comprehensive report on drive health.

Chapter – 21 File System & Disk Usage Analysis

Chapter Overview

This chapter covers essential Linux commands for analyzing disk usage and monitoring file system events. These tools help users manage storage, identify large files and directories, and watch for file changes. Using these utilities allows administrators to optimize storage use, monitor activity, and troubleshoot file system issues efficiently.

Chapter Goal

- Learn to analyze disk usage interactively with ncdu and duf.
- Understand how to monitor file system events with inotifywait.
- Gain skills to view disk space usage in a human-readable format with df -h.

Syntax Table

Serial No	Command	Syntax	Simple Example
1	Disk Usage Analyzer	ncdu [options] [directory]	ncdu /home
2	Disk Usage Utility	duf [options]	duf
3	Monitor Filesystem Events	inotifywait [options] [directory]	inotifywait -m /path/to/watch
4	Display Disk Usage	df -h	df -h

Topic Explanations

1. ncdu - Disk Usage Analyzer with Interactive Text Interface

What is ncdu

The ncdu command is a disk usage analyzer that provides an interactive text interface. It allows users to navigate directories and files by size, helping to quickly identify large files and directories taking up disk space.

Use Purpose

- **Disk Usage Analysis**: Visualizes disk usage and identifies large files.
- **Storage Optimization**: Helps free up disk space by locating unneeded files.

Syntax

```
ncdu [options] [directory]
```

Syntax Explanation

- **ncdu**: Command to analyze disk usage.
  - ○ **[options]**: Configures display, such as -x to stay within one file system.
  - ○ **[directory]**: The directory to analyze (e.g., /home).

Simple Code Example

```
ncdu /home
```

Code Example Explanation

1. **Analyzes** the disk usage of the /home directory, displaying an interactive list of files sorted by size.

Common Errors and Solutions

- **Error**: ncdu: command not found
  - ○ **Solution**: Install ncdu using the package manager (e.g., sudo apt install ncdu).

Notes

- Use arrow keys to navigate, and d to delete files directly from ncdu.

Warnings

- Deleting files directly from ncdu is irreversible; double-check before confirming.

2. duf - Disk Usage Utility with a User-Friendly UI

What is duf

The duf command is a disk usage utility with a user-friendly and colorful interface, displaying mounted file systems, disk usage, and available space. It offers an alternative to the df command with improved readability.

Use Purpose

- **Disk Usage Visualization**: Provides an easy-to-read overview of disk usage.
- **File System Overview**: Displays mounted drives, total capacity, used, and available space.

Syntax

```
duf [options]
```

Syntax Explanation

- **duf**: Command to display disk usage with a user-friendly interface.
    - **[options]**: Configures display, such as -all to show all file systems.

Simple Code Example

```
duf
```

Code Example Explanation

1. **Displays** a colorful and user-friendly overview of all mounted file systems and their usage.

Common Errors and Solutions

- **Error**: duf: command not found
    - **Solution**: Install duf from the package manager or repository.

Notes

- Use duf -only local to display only local file systems and exclude network mounts.

Warnings

- Information displayed may differ from df if some file systems are excluded; double-check if needed.

3. `inotifywait` - Monitor Filesystem Events (Useful for Watching File Changes)

What is `inotifywait`

The `inotifywait` command is part of the `inotify-tools` suite and allows users to monitor file system events, such as file modifications, deletions, or new files. It is useful for real-time monitoring and logging changes in specified directories.

Use Purpose

- **File Change Monitoring**: Watches specified directories for file changes.
- **Real-Time Alerts**: Detects modifications, deletions, and other events as they happen.

Syntax

```
inotifywait [options] [directory]
```

Syntax Explanation

- **inotifywait**: Command to watch file system events.
  - ○ **[options]**: Configures event monitoring, such as -m for continuous monitoring.
  - ○ **[directory]**: The directory to watch for events (e.g., `/path/to/watch`).

Simple Code Example

```
inotifywait -m /path/to/watch
```

Code Example Explanation

1. **Monitors** the `/path/to/watch` directory continuously, displaying file events such as creation, modification, and deletion.

Common Errors and Solutions

- **Error**: `inotifywait: command not found`
  - ○ **Solution**: Install `inotify-tools` using the package manager (e.g., `sudo apt install inotify-tools`).

Notes

- Use specific event flags, like -e modify or -e delete, to monitor only certain types of events.

4. df -h - Display Disk Usage in Human-Readable Format

What is df -h

The df command displays disk usage for file systems, showing used and available space. The -h option presents the information in a human-readable format, using units like KB, MB, or GB for clarity.

Use Purpose

- **Disk Space Summary**: Provides a quick summary of disk usage across file systems.
- **Capacity Monitoring**: Helps track available and used space to prevent full disks.

Syntax

```
df -h
```

Syntax Explanation

- **df**: Command to display disk usage.
    - **-h**: Option to show output in human-readable format (e.g., GB, MB).

Simple Code Example

```
df -h
```

Code Example Explanation

1. **Displays** disk usage of all mounted file systems in human-readable format, showing available, used, and total space.

Common Errors and Solutions

- **Error**: Incorrect output format.
    - **Solution**: Ensure the -h flag is used for human-readable output.

Notes

- Use df -h /path/to/mount to check disk usage for a specific mount point.

Warnings

- Output may include temporary filesystems like tmpfs, which may not reflect actual disk space